DEEP REVISION

DEEP REVISION

A Guide for
Teachers, Students,
and Other Writers

Meredith Sue Willis

Teachers & Writers Collaborative

New York

Deep Revision

The work of Teachers & Writers Collaborative is made possible in part by grants from the New York State Council on the Arts and the National Endowment for the Arts.

Teachers & Writers Collaborative is particularly grateful for support from the following foundations and corporations: The Bingham Trust, American Stock Exchange, The Witter Bynner Foundation for Poetry, Chemical Bank, Consolidated Edison, Aaron Diamond Foundation, The Heckscher Foundation for Children, Morgan Stanley Foundation, New York Telephone, New York Times Company Foundation, Henry Nias Foundation, New York Rotary Foundation of the Rotary Club of New York, Helena Rubinstein Foundation, The Scherman Foundation, and the Lila Wallace-Reader's Digest Fund.

Permissions

The author is grateful for permission to reprint the following material. From *Franz Kafka: The Complete Stories* by Franz Kafka, edited by Nahum N. Glatzer. Copyright 1946, 1947, 1948, 1949, 1954, © 1958, 1971 by Schocken Books, Inc. Reprinted by permission of Schocken Books, published by Pantheon Books, a division of Random House, Inc. "Lying in a Hammock at William Duffy's Farm in Pine Island, Minnesota" by James Wright reprinted from *The Branch Will Not Break* © 1963 by James Wright, Wesleyan University Press. Reprinted by permission of University Press of New England. The poem "Not a tree" by Jane Wilson Joyce is from her book *Beyond the Blue Mountains* published by Gnomon Press and used with their permission. "Autobiography: or How I Grew Up Never Vacationing at Bar Harbor in the Summer" by Peter D. Zivkovic © 1992 is reprinted from *Dog Days* magazine by permission of the author. The zen parables are from *Zen Flesh, Zen Bones* by Paul Reps, published by Charles E. Tuttle, Co., 1957. Reprinted by permission of Charles E. Tuttle, Co.

Teachers & Writers Collaborative
5 Union Square West
New York, N.Y. 10003

Library of Congress Cataloging-in-Publication Data

Willis, Meredith Sue.
Deep Revision : a guide for teachers, students, and other writers / by Meredith Sue Willis.
    p.   cm.
Includes bibliographical references.
ISBN 0-915924-40-4. — ISBN 0-915924-41-2 (paper)
1. English language—Composition and exercises—Study and teaching (Secondary). 2. English language—Rhetoric. 3. English language—Style. 4. Editing. I. Title.
LB1631.W45   1993
808'.042'0712—dc20

                            93-1524
                            CIP

Printed by Philmark Lithographics, New York, N.Y.

Sixth printing

This book is dedicated to the memory of
Sherry Weinberger
who made *mother-in-law* mean *friend.*

Table of Contents

How to Use This Book

An underlying thesis of *Deep Revision* is that all phases of writing, including revision, have a great deal in common across age groups and levels of accomplishment. This idea comes from my experience as a teacher of writing to children, adolescents, college students, and adults, and as a writer and member of a writers' peer group. I am convinced that the heart of what happens in writing is shared by all writers, professional and avocational, adult and child.

I am further convinced that drafting and revising are at many points so closely intertwined that it is impossible to tell them apart. I might draft a chapter of this book, and then, as I begin to revise it, come up with a whole new passage that I need to add. What do I call this kind of writing? I am not polishing or editing, but re-seeing my original material by coming up with entirely new material. My revising thus includes new drafting in the service of going farther, going deeper.

Because *Deep Revision* is meant to be a practical book, it has many activities to encourage and develop this process. The exercises include things to try by yourself and things to do in a group or with a class. The activities are indicated by **TRY THIS.** Many of these exercises are appropriate for anyone who writes. A few are particularly useful for adults (how to structure a book-length manuscript, for example) or young children (using drawing as a way to revise), but all of the exercises have the general aim of deepening, developing, and tightening what we write. Many of the exercises could also be used for getting started or restarted.

The book includes numerous examples, with discussions of how the examples have been revised. My intention is to show many possible approaches to getting deeper into writing. Generally speaking, within each chapter there is an advance from basic ideas toward more complex and sophisticated ones. Part I looks at how the ability to revise develops, and at how people can use one another's responses to improve their writing. Part II offers techniques for adding more material and deepening the material you have, and Part III is about form, structure, and finishing.

I have used many people's suggestions in this book, and, wherever possible, I credit them directly. Some ideas, however, are developed simultaneously by many people, and I know that some of my writing exercises are far from unique. Because most of these techniques came to me in the course of giving writing workshops, my first thanks are due to the people I have been privileged to learn from by teaching—adults, young people, and children. Their enthusiasm and experimentation have given me ideas and an opportunity to try out the ideas.

A number of institutions have given financial backing directly and indirectly for my writing workshops: New York University (where I developed and teach two courses called Beginning Your Novel and Structuring Your Novel); the National Endowment for the Arts; the New Jersey State Council on the Arts; the Morris Area Arts Council; the Newark Project of the Essex Arts Council; Project Impact; and Teachers & Writers Collaborative. I also want to thank my students from the Expository Writing Tutorial by Mail course, part of the program of the Center for Talented Youth at Johns Hopkins University.

Certain friends and colleagues have gone beyond the call of duty in sharing their ideas on revision. Among them are my sister Christine Willis, who teaches English at Arroyo Grande High School in Arroyo Grande, California; Chris Schorr at Chatham High School in Chatham, New Jersey; Edna Patton at James Caldwell High School in West Caldwell, New Jersey; Sandra Prince at Clinton School in Maplewood, New Jersey; my friend and colleague Suzanne McConnell, who teaches at Hunter College in New York City; Jane Wilson Joyce, the poet and scholar; Tom Douglass, writer and scholar of Appalachian literature; the past and present members of my writers' group—Sybil Claiborne, Carol Emshwiller, Ingrid Hughes, Eva Kollisch, Suzanne McConnell, Charlotte Meehan, Kate Riley, Carole Rosenthal, and Vera B. Williams; and, of course, my husband Andy Weinberger and my son Joel Howard Willis Weinberger.

PART ONE

◆

THINKING ABOUT REVISION

Chapter One

A Look at Some Revised Pieces

You hand a manuscript to a teacher or a boss or an editor and wait nervously for a response. The paper comes back with marks on it: corrections, queries, suggestions, little notes of praise or criticism. I begin this book on revision with the image of two people and a manuscript because the experience is familiar, and because it is a way of beginning with concrete examples of revision.

Every writer has a personal anecdote: for me, there was the teacher who said I could be a writer; there was the one who bracketed my purple passages and taught me to cut; and there was also the one who bloodied my personal experience with red ink. There is a perhaps apocryphal story of the editor of a little magazine who blew his nose on the first page of a manuscript and mailed it back; there is the rejection letter that included a suggestion that turned the rejected manuscript into one that was published.

We don't always remember the precise teaching or editing technique that improved our writing, but we remember the teacher or editor. Teaching is nothing if not a personal art: lectures can be brilliant, fascinating, and full of insight, but they are, in the end, a performance. The great lecturer's audience learns and is inspired, but the art of lecturing is different from the art of teaching, which is constantly modified by the student's responses and the student's own work.

Chris Schorr, a high school English teacher in Chatham, New Jersey, says, "A fuzzy area that I think about *a lot* is how much the success a writing teacher has is dependent on how generally good the relationship is between the student and the teacher. I can't critique a kid's paper if I'm mad at him or her—we have to like each other while we're doing the work together because taking criticism is really hard."

It's difficult to describe this very important and delicate back-and-forth between two individuals, or among members of a group, that results in changes in the writing. Often in this book, I discuss the writer revising in solitude, but for many people at many stages of their writing, what is most useful is the interaction with other people.

To younger children, the first thing a teacher needs to convey is that the students' ideas are valid, and the second is that what they write can be changed. This profound and liberating realization can come early or late. Ron Padgett, a poet and editor, says:

> When I was little, writing things for school, I assumed I had to accept whatever words came into my head: those were the words I would write down for the teacher. That is, my writing mode was passive. Concomitant was the feeling that whatever I said in a poem or essay had to express what I "really" felt. In other words, I had almost no control over the entire process.

To grow accustomed to making changes and working one's way back into a piece is to be well on the way to serious, deep revision. The concept that every utterance or production (by child or adult) is perfect in its spontaneity seems at best doubtful. Children, like adult writers, want their work to be treated with interest and respect, to be shared with others and enjoyed, but a child in a supportive classroom with an appreciative teacher learns that making changes can be a positive experience, even fun: you can add things, take away things, make a second draft, get ideas from a partner, turn a description into a story, turn a story into a play, turn a play into an opera. It is atmosphere and attitude that count here.

Jason was a first grader who, his teacher informed me, had moved to town well after school started, and was about to move again. He lagged behind the other children in his skills. One day he drew a picture of a rocket (although the other children were following my instruction to write first and illustrate afterward). Then he wrote this:

> spase shuttle and he is
> etaing

I had very little idea of what Jason was writing about, except "spase shuttle" (he had asked me for the spelling), so I asked him to read back to me what he had written, and found out that the lines said "He is on a space shuttle and he is eating." I said, "Tell me more," and Jason explained that the astronaut was doing a lot of things in space, experimenting and eating meals. He was very happy to talk about his piece, and in fact kept right on talking. He told me that one of the experiments they were doing on the space shuttle was with a Slinky toy, and also that the astronauts hear banging in space. I said, "That's interesting, Jason. I'd like you to write that, so that if you weren't here to tell me, I could read it on your paper." This made sense to Jason, as it does to most kids. His revised version read:

> spase shuttle and he is
> etaing he sees a slickey
> and he heres baine
> ///////////
> /////////

On my next visit to his desk, he explained that the banging was meteorites hitting the walls and the marks at the bottom were meteorites. Jason's piece is typical of writers at his level—their knowledge and imaginative powers are far ahead of their ability to write, even *with* invented spelling and receptive adults around. There are many ways of using this information: you can take dictation from the children or they can work again on the same piece, adding as many of the spoken sentences as possible. In the early weeks of first grade, the students' drawings are considered part of the communication.[1] Every moment is rich with potential revision: Jason adds more orally, then writes in response to the adult's response to what he says. He makes a picture, he darkens some of his words for emphasis. When he takes his turn reading aloud to the class, he adds still more ideas. This back-and-forth, making adjustments, is what younger children do all the time in everyday life. They can learn to do it in writing as well.

The child learning to revise finds ways of assimilating adult suggestions. This doesn't mean slavishly making whatever changes the teacher suggests, but thinking over the suggestions and using whatever enhances the student's own ideas. I asked a class of fourth graders to do an exercise in which they close their eyes and picture an object, animate or inanimate, the only rule being that it should be something small enough to hold in their hands. I asked them to imagine the thing, to feel it, smell it, hear it, and even (we got good laughs out of this) taste it, if that seemed appropriate. One student wrote:

---

[1] For more on revision with young children, see chapter two.

> It is a worm, and it is slimy and smells like mud and it is long and skinny whith no teeth or ears or nose. It is brown and about 2 or 3 inches long. It is ugly and slithery and grose and not to many people like them.
>
> —*Sam Edge*

As I walked around looking at the students' work, I read Sam's piece over his shoulder. I ignored the spelling and punctuation and responded out of my own personal interests, which included a vegetable garden. I said to Sam, "That's pretty vivid, with the slimy and slithery. But, by the way, they're good, you know, worms."

"Why?" said Sam, with narrowed eye.

"They make dirt." I controlled my urge to extol the virtues of organic soil improvement. "If not for earthworms, we probably couldn't have good soil to grow vegetables."

Then I drifted away to see what the other kids had written. After having a few students read aloud, I gave the next part of the assignment, which was to make up something about the object. We talked about different kinds of fiction—that it can be realistic or fantastic. I told the students that the only requirement was that they make something happen to their object that hadn't·happened to it in real life.

When I came by the next time, Sam's piece read:

> It is a worm, and it is slimy and smells like mud and it is long and skinny whith no teeth or ears or nose. It is brown and about 2 or 3 inches long. It is ugly and slithery and grose and not to many people like them.
>
> What if a worm was pretty and smelled like flowers and had bluish eyes with smooth and dryish skin. It wouldn't want to go in the soil and the dirt would be to hard even to shuvl.

Sam had used my little speech about worms directly in his writing. He used fictional speculation on what continued to be a nonfiction piece. Everything was grist for his mill, and he, like younger students, was quite ready to incorporate any friendly advice from others, children and adults alike.

Often in my workshops as a writer-in-the-schools, I feel hampered by the lack of sustained periods of time with the same students. When

I do have time to look at a piece of writing over an extended period of time, it is usually in a college or adult class. I respond on occasion to whole novels of former students, and I like that very much—to read a large work and talk about structure and plot. I also had the opportunity to work with middle school students for an extended period of time through the Johns Hopkins Expository Center for Talented Youth. I taught an Expository Writing Tutorial by Mail (EWT), in which the entire teacher-student interaction happened on paper. I would make my notes on their papers (usually brief comments such as "Wow" and "Do you think you could come up with a better opening line?") and also write letters on matters of deeper revision. The students did the assignments, revised, and often told me about school and extracurricular activities, in lively personal letters. The following is a somewhat shortened version of one of these exchanges near the beginning of the course:

October 18

Dear Jen,

My name is Meredith Sue Willis, and I will be your tutor for the Expository Writing Tutorial of the Center for Talented Youth at Johns Hopkins University. I am a professional writer, having published three novels, two books of nonfiction, and many short stories, articles, and book reviews. I also enjoy teaching: I give writing workshops in public schools, and I teach a course for adults at New York University in New York City called "Beginning Your Novel." I also give workshops for teachers about how to help students write better. I live with my husband, who is a physician, and my little boy, who just started kindergarten.

Writing is useful for me—I write to tell you your assignments for this course, for example—but writing for me is also deeply enjoyable and very difficult. The whole point of this tutorial, of course, is to improve your writing skills. I have three secrets for doing this. First: read as much as you can, especially the work of excellent writers. Second: write often and as much as you can. The third secret is to find some way to make the writing you do interesting to yourself. You can wash dishes without being terribly interested and still get the dishes clean, but writing well when you don't care about what you write is almost impossible. This is because writing, whether it's a joke you are telling your pen pal or a serious diary entry, comes out of *you*.

I hope you will find a way to make each assignment in this tutorial interesting to yourself—and to me!

Assignment

TRY THIS: This assignment is a "place" writing. One of the most important things to learn to do in writing is to find a way to put what you have in your mind into another person's mind. One of the best ways to do this is with the five senses. The reason the senses work so well is that most human beings can see, hear, smell, taste and touch—and even people without one sense have others.

To begin the assignment, close your eyes and slowly, in your imagination, recreate a place you have been. It can be indoors or outdoors, a place you like or—maybe even better—a place you hate or have serious reservations about. In your imagination, put yourself there. Start with sounds: is it noisy? Is there music? Are people talking? Do you hear birds? Is there a sound of water? Take a deep breath in your imagination, and breathe in the air of the place. What odors does it have? Can you smell something cooking? Is there something to taste? In your imagination, feel the air of the place: is there a breeze, is it hot, cold? Touch some things with your fingers too: are there soft things, hard, feathery? Finally, in your imagination, look around the place. Use your senses to explore the place as long as you want, then write as much as you can of what you experienced with your eyes closed. Try to get all five senses in, but don't worry if there's no taste. Tell it however you'd like ("In my place . . . " or "I looked around me . . . " or "First I heard the sound of . . . " or whatever). Try to get in as many different sense impressions as you can.

What I am looking for is a description of a place that makes me feel like I've been there. Good luck! Don't forget, this is due very soon—October 29.

That is a lot for this first letter from me! Well, Jen, I look forward to receiving your assignment on October 29, and learning more about you.

Sincerely,
Sue

October 21

Dear Sue,

I wasn't quite sure if I should call you Sue. You signed the letter that way, but everywhere else it said Meredith. So, if you have any preference, please tell me. When I received your letter yesterday, I couldn't stop talking about it. Never in my life did I think I was going to be tutored by a professional writer!

Well, you want to know something about me. I'm an only child, and my favorite pastime is writing stories. I'm in eighth grade and in my last year in middle school. I like Language Arts, but I would like it a lot more if we did some creative writing. This year we learn mostly grammar and vocabulary. I guess I can't complain too much, because last year in Language Arts we would come into class, get our writing folders, and write for forty-five minutes almost every day! I loved it!

I also like to read and play the piano. This year I am on the eighth grade field hockey team and I really enjoy it. So far we are undefeated. As much as I like hockey, I like tennis a lot more.

I love your secrets for successful writing. I don't think I should have a problem with them since I love to read, and therefore I do it often. My mom encourages me to read novels written by excellent writers and I enjoy it. I also love to write. (I think I already told you that.) It usually depends on the topic of what I'm writing in order for it to be interesting to me. Even if I don't like the topic, I can usually make it more interesting to write about by adding dialogue, or writing it through the eyes of someone else.

Thanks for the tips!

> Sincerely,
> Jen Colaguori

*   *   *   *   *

Rose's Dollhouse Goodies

Three steps down and you're in a different world. Everything you could possibly think of that is found in your own house is reproduced and found in Rose's Dollhouse Goodies, only an inch to a foot scale. This small, one room shop has a distinct atmosphere of its own.

When you walk down the steps and into the shop, it's almost guaranteed that you will hear the phone ringing. The phone usually drowns out the hum of the soft classical music in the background, but if you strain hard enough, you might be able to hear it. This store is not one that is full of commotion. The people whispering, asking questions, raving about the "little things," and the steady rhythm of the saw suggest a quiet atmosphere.

Immediately the smell of paint, wood, and sawdust will come to your senses. A musty aroma fills the room, almost like the one of a basement or attic, only this has more of a distinct smell of cigarettes. The dampness smells like the taste of stale bread.

This workshop type of store does not have a breeze. The air is perfectly still and it is neither hot nor cold. Everything here has a different feel to it. For example, the miniature carpets are soft, the flooring is hard, the shingles are rough, the bathroom furniture is cold and smooth, and the bedroom furniture feels as if it would be very comfortable to sit in. On the living room furniture, the small, elegant details are distinct.

The first thought you have when you enter Rose's is, "What happened here?" It looks as though someone took her shop and shook it. Everything you could imagine is scattered everywhere. Some items are in boxes, on shelves, in cases, or not neatly stacked in piles on the floor. The items are small, but since there are many of them, they seem to take up space. This shop does not have much lighting which therefore gives it a dreary atmosphere. Rose, the owner of the store, is a permanent fixture. As a matter of fact, she fits right in. She's of medium height, has pale skin, and white hair. She has a ragged look about her, a deep gravelly voice, and there is never a time that she doesn't look tired.

It's true that you have entered another world once you take the three steps down into Rose's Dollhouse Goodies. All of this put together helps make it a unique store.

—*Jen Colaguori*

*   *   *   *   *

November 1

Dear Jen,

Thanks for the interesting and enthusiastic letter! The letters are really important to me, since we don't meet. I'm glad to hear you are an athlete as well as a creative writer—when I was a kid, they didn't organize a lot of sports for girls, and I always felt deprived. So now I swim and run and do as much as I can out-of-doors.

"Rose's Dollhouse Goodies" sounds like an intriguing place. So intriguing, in fact, that the next assignment is going to be a revision of it. I'm starting right off with a revision assignment because I think it is almost the most important stage of writing. Most of my writing, I have to say, is revising. I usually sit down and draft out my ideas as quickly and sloppily as possible, and then go back and start doing the real work.

I won't go over all the little suggestions I made on your paper, but I wanted to talk about a big suggestion, which is that in some ways, the most interesting part of the essay was how you seem both fascinated by Rose's (and by Rose herself!) and at the same time a little put off by the mess, the cigarette smells, and Rose's ragged look. Can you get this mixed feeling into the paper from the very beginning? Something about all the perfection of the little things, but also the disorder? Perhaps if you mentioned ragged, tired Rose early on, you could do this. Perhaps also you could give a sample of her dialogue, as you say you like to do in your nonfiction writing as well as in your fiction writing.

Your choice of sense details is excellent—I really enjoyed those smells and sounds and feels. Also, while the essay itself is very interesting, the final paragraph sounds like something you tagged on as a "conclusion." Everything in the essay is interesting, but the conclusion is pretty dull. Can't you conclude (if you feel you need to sum it all up) with something about your favorite thing in the store, or the best thing or worst thing about it, or maybe even your mixed feelings?

Mostly, I want to see how you get back into a piece you've already written. I am really looking forward to seeing more of your writing, Jen!

Sincerely,
Sue

*　　*　　*　　*　　*

Rose's Dollhouse Goodies (revised)

Three steps down and you're in a different world. Everything you could possibly think of that is found in your own house is reproduced and found in Rose's Dollhouse Goodies, only an inch to a foot scale. This small, one room shop has a distinct atmosphere of its own. You can't spend any time there without having mixed feelings about the store. If you love miniatures, it's a wonderful place to browse, but the atmosphere could make the experience less pleasant.

The first thought you have when you enter Rose's is, "What happened here?" It looks as though someone took her shop and shook it. Everything you could imagine is scattered everywhere. Some items are in boxes, on shelves, in cases, or stacked in messy piles on the floor. The items are small, but since there are many of them, they seem to take up space and give the store a cluttered look. This shop does not have much lighting, which, therefore, gives it a dreary atmosphere.

When you walk down the steps and into the shop, it's almost guaranteed that you will hear the phone ringing. The phone usually drowns out the hum of the soft classical music in the background, but if you strain hard enough, you might be able to hear it. The deep gravelly voice of Rose, the owner, will greet you with a simple "Hi," although her presence is always hidden at first. Once she does appear from the mess strewn across the store, you will see that she is of medium height, has pale skin, and white straggly hair. This adds to her ragged, tired look, which matches the general disarray of the store and its atmosphere. A typical statement from Rose that you would hear upon entering is, "Oh, I'm still waiting for those shingles . . ." She would then start to fish through a pile of papers, which makes you wonder if she ever in fact placed the order. This store is not one that is full of commotion. The people whispering, asking questions, raving about the "little things," and the steady rhythm of the saw suggest a quiet atmosphere.

Immediately the smell of paint, wood, and sawdust will come to your senses. A musty aroma fills the room, almost like the one of a basement or attic, only this has more of a distinct smell of cigarettes. The dampness smells like the taste of stale bread.

This store does not have a breeze. The air is perfectly still and it is neither hot nor cold. Everything here has a different feel to it. For example, the miniature carpets are soft like fur, the flooring is hard and stiff as cardboard, the shingles are rough, grooved pieces of wood, the bathroom furniture is cold and smooth like a sheet of metal, and the bedroom furniture feels as if it would be very comfortable to sit in. On the living room furniture, the small, elegant details are distinct and intricately carved.

One of my favorite pastimes is to browse and explore in Rose's Dollhouse Goodies. Because I love to admire and collect miniatures for my dollhouse, I find that this unique store fascinates me. It is the general disarray of the shop that I find disconcerting. It seems to be a contradiction how everything in this store could be made to such perfection, but be displayed in such a disorganized manner.

—*Jen Colaguori*

*   *   *   *   *

November 30

Dear Jen,

The second draft of "Rose's" is a lot better. The ending is a big improvement, and I like the second paragraph and the paragraph where you wonder if Rose really ordered the shingles. At one point, though, I felt that you were using the old draft without really making it fit in. After describing Rose, you go right into "This store is not full of commotion." That certainly needs to be in a separate paragraph. Also, the smells are no longer "immediately" because we're well into the second half of the essay.

Overall, though, I am delighted by the way you really went into the essay and moved things around, added things, and came up with a much better ending. It's easy enough to change a word or phrase the teacher suggests to you, and much harder to reorganize as you have done here. Harder, but, in my humble opinion, more fun. The suggestions I'm making here are just in case you want to do a third draft for a later assignment in this course, or for some school assignment.

I hope your big weekend with your Long Island and Cherry Hill friends went well. I'll be looking forward to seeing your personal narrative—and enjoy your holidays!

Sincerely,
Sue

Jen liked being edited and responded to my suggestions with alacrity and enthusiasm. I too love to have a sympathetic person with a sincere interest in improving my work go over it. In order to have this, I have sought out a group of writers I meet with regularly for hearing and critiquing each others' writing. I went through a time in my life when I wrote alone, not showing my work to anyone, and I would hate to return to that—it is *so* important to have other people read your work. Sure, they make excellent suggestions, but they also simply receive it, are there to hear what I am saying.

Revision in class is trickier, of course, especially for teachers who are not working with enthusiastic eighth graders like Jen Colaguori—but still want to create a good atmosphere for revision. How do you do serious work in a classroom where attendance is mandatory and the students are not particularly committed to writing? The students may even have gross misconceptions about revision: my sister Christine Willis, a high school English teacher in California, told her class that when something is important, she will rewrite it twelve or thirteen times, and one boy responded, "But, Mrs. Willis, you must be very inaccurate!"

Students may be working at wildly different levels of ability and interest, and, especially with adolescents, life outside the classroom occupies most of their thoughts. Also, I find myself wondering how personal activities such as writing and revising take place in a classroom anyhow. It never fails to amaze me, when I think about it, that students do as well as they do when teachers say, "Okay, folks, lunch is over, the bell rang. Let's get to work on revising the Most Embarrassing Experiences we started yesterday." Imagine the effort it takes to move from the thrill of finally making eye contact with the person you've been admiring for six weeks—to the task of revising. How to give revision even the tiniest scintilla of value compared to real life? How to encourage even a little self-motivation in revision?

Chris Schorr, the high school English teacher I quoted earlier, does it by giving revision pride of place in her plan for the whole year's work. In her class, revision is not an afterthought or for extra credit, it is at the heart of her writing program. "Generally speaking," she says, "revision exercises have to be short . . . and they have to be targeted—e.g., verb improvement, use of a simile/metaphor, concrete detail, or whatever." Furthermore, "Those purposes have to be clearly visible before you start, and clearly measurable—student readers have to be able to recognize the changes in each other's papers, and to check them off a list." Chris uses peer response and peer editing at all stages of revision in her classroom, and she gives students credit for the *process* of responding and revising as well as the final draft, or else, she says, the students won't go through it.

Invited to Chris Schorr's classroom as a visiting writer for three days, I assigned some point-of-view exercises (see chapter eight), including one in which you describe a character from the outside, emphasizing physical detail, and then describe the character from the inside, by writing an imaginary internal monologue.[2] Chris and her tenth grade students then revised their drafts, culminating in a booklet of the students' revisions. Matt Moreno's piece started in class like this:

> His name is Mr. Teacher. He smells like an ice cream parlor due to his vanilla cologne. His ties are horrendous but yet he is still in fashion. His attitude is odd, because of his moral thoughts. The way he speaks is very intelligent and he knows his subject well. His sense of humor is hidden, and only a keen person could find it. Mr. Teacher stands up for what he believes in and is not afraid to show his belief. Also, his light voice is young, but his thoughts are old and wise. He's not the type to give a pat-on-the-back but will show you right in a small but satisfying way. I'm impressed with Mr. Teacher's beard because it's always short and not super hairy. When he teaches, we learn, we don't just get entertained.

---

[2] For a fuller description of how this exercise works as revision, see chapter seven, "Revising Fiction."

Monologue:
Another day of hell with these kids. I enjoy teaching but it's not fair that they don't enjoy learning. How can kids like this help steer the country to the fate it wants to be in, and not the fate it's heading. I seem selfish when I say this, but if I don't say this, then there's no chance for changes. I feel sorry for them because they will see what happens to each other and they won't like it. If they come for help I wouldn't know where to start. I may just need help from them.

—*Matt Moreno, tenth grade*

I thought it was a pretty good piece as it stood—the "outer" description was perhaps a bit too much like a list, but he did pull it together at the end, and I particularly liked the monologue. Later, however, Chris put the students through her rigorous process of revising. She described what the students did for their revisions:

First we talked again (I talked mostly) about the difference between "telling" (not good) and "showing," and I put a list of signs-that-you're-not-"showing" on the board:

1. Are all your sentences about the same length and built the same way? For example, The _____ is _____. She has ____ ____. This is a bad sign. It's boring.

2. What kind of verbs do you have and what tense are they in? Are they mostly helping verbs? Are they all in past or progressive tenses? If you answered yes, this is a bad sign. It's boring.

3. How many of the reader's senses have you involved? If your whole description sounds like a police blotter entry—this is a sign that you're telling, not showing, and it's boring.

4. How specific are your details? Words like *pretty* or *nice* or *beautiful* tell about you, not your subject. If that's the kind of description you're offering, this also gets boring.

There are ten commandments of good writing. The first nine are, "Thou shalt not be dull."

Chris then asked her students to mark all the places they thought they had broken the commandments. Then, of course, they were to fix up the marked areas. The last step they did in pairs, checking one another's papers and making other suggestions, but also pointing out the things they thought were especially effective. Chris read through their final drafts quickly, complimenting what she thought was effective and pointing out the parts she thought didn't work, often because the detail wasn't concrete or specific enough. She gave the students half credit for getting to this stage, and the other half when they brought in the typed paragraph. She finds that the kids really benefit from this kind of intense examination, especially in their verb choices and use of detail, and she can see this in subsequent assignments.

Here is Matt Moreno's piece after this in-class revision process:

His name is Mr. Teacher. The first thing a person notices about him is his vanilla-scented aftershave. Another thing someone notices is his fashion in ties. His ties are very outrageous, yet still in style. One of his ties has tessellations of postage stamps. The tie itself has lime green and hot pink fluorescent colors. Another tie has a picture of Oriental people and some Oriental writing. The colors on this tie are an off-white base with black writing. To add to this strangeness he occasionally wears a bow tie (but only with suspenders). His beard (and what a beard he has) is always trimmed to the geometry of his face. The beard never grows under his chin. It is on the jawline from one sideburn to the other. A moustache goes with it also. It's brown with gray hairs scattered around. Mr. Teacher seems like a man with a shy attitude. He doesn't like to express his feelings unless someone asks him to. Then he is very straightforward and to the point. The only feelings he seems to show are his feelings towards his religion. He takes his religion very seriously and once said, "If a student ever came into my class wearing a swastika on his shirt, I would physically remove him myself!" His father was a rabbi and Mr. Teacher grew up to follow his religion very strictly. Another quality Mr. Teacher has is his hidden sense of humor. He'll never tell a joke or make fun of someone, but somehow he makes you laugh. When he was teaching the War of 1812 he was making fun of the Americans and British for fighting. The whole war could have been prevented if it weren't for the delay of information caused by a month-long journey of a ship. Mr. Teacher said, "The war would have been prevented by a FAX." Mr. Teacher is very accomplished and a person who has earned the respect of peers and students. He's a powerful teacher.

In choice of detail and elaboration, Matt has improved his portrait a great deal. The description, especially of Mr. Teacher's appearance, manages to be both humorous and affectionate. The elaborate description of ties is quite amusing, and an excellent example of what Chris Schorr and I and most other teachers of writing would agree is the reason for more details. Instead of the imagined interior monologue, Matt now sticks to nonfiction, relating observations about history that Mr. Teacher has made and giving the reader some interesting background on Mr. Teacher's family and his passionate connection with Judaism. What was an experiment in extending description into fiction has now developed into an excellent nonfiction portrait. The revision is fuller and deeper through vivid, concrete, amusing details, relevant background, and dramatization through direct quotation.

I have to say I miss the imagined monologue, which certainly doesn't fit into the revised composition (after all, that was *my* contribution to the assignment), but even though Matt chose to cut the monologue, my guess is that the experience of writing it probably deepened his revision. There is also no reason why Matt couldn't, if he chose, use the same material more than once—in fiction and in nonfiction. I am fond of the idea of using the same material in both an essay form (as Matt ultimately did) and in fiction, and often find myself doing this in my own work. Sometimes I do this only to make certain I have found the right form, sometimes I actually make more than one finished version.

TRY THIS: Take some piece of nonfiction you have written recently—a letter, a memo or report for work, a journal entry—and make a list of ideas for how you might use the same material. Could the point you make in a letter-to-the-editor be used in a parable? Might the description in an article become the setting for a mystery story? Does the work report suggest a funny situation that might become a comedy sketch for television? Try to come up with at least five possibilities.

TRY THIS: Choose one and draft it.

TRY THIS: Try another one!

Chris Schorr puts a lot of emphasis on what she calls "redos." Unless a piece is a test, she allows students to rewrite and resubmit any essay as often as they want during a term, and they always get the new grade on the assignment. She says that of all the things she has tried, this method leads to the best revisions because it doesn't penalize kids for learning how to write well. Including rewrites in the general plan for grading seems to me both practical and essential if you really want to teach students to revise. To me, the idea of getting back a paper marked up and commented on and even graded, and then having no recourse—no chance to respond to these communications—is lunacy. What good are comments on a piece of writing if they aren't used in another round of revision? Final editing for publication works back and forth this way (you give me feedback, I make changes based on your suggestions, you make further comments), and so does an early response from a friend. The same kind of interaction happens with so-called creative or artistic writing as it does with briefs being drafted in a law office. The movement is back and forth, from one person to another.

Andrew Chu was a senior engineering student at Cooper Union for the Advancement of the Arts and Sciences, a four-year college, when he took my creative writing course. The course was an elective, and while he was certainly interested in making a good grade, he was very open to trying things he hadn't done before, partly because his field of expertise was elsewhere. Andrew was quite willing to make as many drafts as I felt necessary; in fact, he usually made more. Part of the course covered poetry writing—something of an experiment for me, as I am primarily a fiction writer. Andrew became fascinated by poetic forms. He wrote a couple of elaborately rhymed Shakespearean sonnets. The assignment in the example below, however, was to write a poem following some particular rhythm of your own choice, and he decided to practice iambic tetrameter: ta-DAH ta-DAH ta-DAH ta-DAH.

Just Another Day

It's just another day at home.
I sit alone atop the steps.
Bright red IROCs go cruising by
Tunes blaring, careless talk abounds.
Old men collecting soda cans
Content to find just 10 a day.
School kids running, playing, shouting.
No worries, save what to eat, to drink.

God knows I shouldn't be depressed.
Why shouldn't you enjoy yourself?
For Father pays the room and board,
Mom cooks and cleans and washes dishes.

You self-centered son of a bitch.
6 million people starve each day
and all you do is sulk and moan
for unrequited lust that was a dream.

It's now 2 years since our paths crossed
1 year 10 months 9 days 2 hours
to be exact. Ah, what a day.
The date I found out we were 2, not 1.

At present sunset's breaking fast.
Kids return home, the men go drink.
Perhaps I'll set the table now
for want of something else to do.
Next week I'll go to church and pray
that God will grant me strength to say
"I'm doing great, I got it all."

It's just another day at home.

My first comments focused predictably on clarifying, adding details, and tightening the language. "Very nice," I scribbled on the margin. "Kept the iambic tetrameter very well. A few places you could tighten—get rid of connecting words. Also—what are IROCs? What kind of steps, too? A stoop? A private house? Apartment? You need to add a few details to ground the reader."

The day I handed back the poems, we had a session of peer editing in small groups, and Andrew and three classmates sat on the floor in the hall and passed their poems around, adding comments that were even fuller than mine. Like me, they didn't know what IROCs were (a type of Ford Mustang). "Kill the IROCs," was one student's comment. "Maybe 'cars' or a more generic car." The same student suggested, "In the third stanza, you're not descriptive like the others (6 million people, counting each day . . .). Maybe add more numbers . . . something about the room and board, in numbers." One peer editor didn't like "son of a bitch," saying, "I'm not crazy about this line. Perhaps it's strong enough to stand on its own, or maybe put it as the last line in the stanza instead of the first. Or maybe the description is descriptive enough without the harsh words." Andrew did ultimately decide to get rid of it, coming up instead with "self-centered little prince," which I think is a lot better—

after all, S.O.B. reflects badly on one's mother, hardly the point of his poem.

Andrew's revision went like this:

Just Another Day

It's just another day at home.
I sit atop the stoop, alone.
A bright red Mustang cruises by
Tunes blaring, careless talk abounds.

Old men collecting soda cans
Content to find just 10 a day.
School boys running, playing, shouting.   [Or: A Coke, a Sprite, or ginger ale.
No worries, save what to eat and drink.   2 hot dogs, burgers, maybe fries.]

God knows I shouldn't be depressed.
Why shouldn't I enjoy myself?
Our father pays the rent, 1 grand.
Mom cooks, and cleans, and scrubs the john.

6 million people starve each day
and all I do is sulk and moan
for unrequited lust—a dream.
Self-centered little prince, that's me.

It's now 2 years since our paths crossed
1 year 10 months 9 days 2 hours
to be exact. Ah, what a day.
The date I found out we were 2, not 1.

At present sunset's breaking fast.
The kids come home, the men go drink.
Perhaps I'll set the table now
for want of something else to do.

Next week I'll go to church and pray
that God will grant me strength to say
"I'm doing great, I got it all."

It's just another day at home.

This time, I responded, "I'd like to see you give this one more go round soon—I think you should definitely stay with the four-line stanzas *and* the tetrameter. The little squares of short stanzas fit the trapped mood."

The last version—at least the one he turned in, because he was clearly still tinkering with the poem—went like this:

Just Another Day

It's just another day at home.
I sit atop the stoop, alone.
A bright red Mustang cruises by
with music blaring, talk abounds.

Old men collecting soda cans
Content to find just 10 a day.
A dozen school boys run and shout
They worry not, just play all day.

God knows I shouldn't be depressed.
Why shouldn't I enjoy myself?
Our father pays the rent, 1 grand.
Mom cooks, and cleans, and scrubs the john.

6 million people starve each day
and all I do is sulk and moan
for unrequited lust—a dream.
Self-centered little prince, that's me.

It's now 2 years since our paths crossed
1 year 10 months 9 days 2 hours
to be exact. Recall that day.
["Alternate: to be exact. I loathe that day," wrote Andrew.]
The date I found out we were 2, not 1.

"I'm sure you've heard this line before,
but truly this is how I feel.
Your heart is pure, your virtue deep.
I wish I could reciprocate."

At present sunset's breaking fast.
The kids come home, the men go drink.
Perhaps I'll set the table now
for want of something else to do.

Next week I'll go to church and pray
that God will grant me strength to say
"I'm doing great, I got it all."
It's just another day at home.

"Note," Andrew wrote, "the new quotation is also an experiment. I would rather have an even number of stanzas, either six or eight. I was thinking of cutting the sunset stanza but added this instead (sigh). There always seems to be something new to improve."

I responded, "It *is* eight stanzas, right? The quotation is excellent. Lay it aside a while, then go over it again—time often smoothes writing, for me anyhow. This poem has been a real pleasure to follow!"

There is really nothing more fun, if you enjoy the art of language, than editing and being edited. To talk about language, not abstractly, not in awed worship of Great Works but in a collaborative act of making. Teaching and editing demand the participation of the other person. Helping someone revise in this way is at once as concrete as sewing a seam or planting a seed and as important as any human exploration of experience and communication of feeling. I love good editing, whether it is done by me or to me.

Bad editing, of course, is unspeakably infuriating. I remember once when my editor at Scribner's turned over my manuscript to an outside copy editor who changed all of my dashes and a lot of my periods into ellipses, giving a whole different tone to the novel. I was furious. The editor was more controlled but equally unimpressed with the changes. The ellipses were erased by hand by my poor editor, and the copy editor not used again. Everyone who has been a student or a published writer has some such story—a reader or teacher or editor who did something incredibly stupid to a manuscript. I don't like to think about it, but I know that from time to time I must have inadvertently written something on a student's paper that was the opposite of helpful. This is one more reason not to mark in red every tiny error in a beginning writer's work. Part of the teacher-editor's goal should be to make revision an interesting experience that both parties are fully involved in. Revision need not be a painful procedure best blocked out and forgotten. There needs to be some congruity between what the teacher or editor is correcting and what the writer both wants to achieve and *is capable of achieving at a given time.*

There are some lyric poems in which every word is precisely the right word in precisely the right place, and there are possibly short stories and short essays of similar perfection, but you will be hard pressed to show me a book, nonfiction or fiction, that could not benefit from one last go-through for changes. My case in point is that I once gave a reading from my work on the same platform as Irini Spanidou, a marvelous stylist whose book *God's Snake* has been praised highly and justly for the power of its language. That evening, she arrived with the published book in hand, open to the chapter she intended to read. The printed pages were covered with her penciled changes: she was still polishing, years after the novel had been published, praised, and reprinted.

Spanidou is an artist—never completely satisfied, always trying to make her work better—but the anecdote also points up something that is liberating to me as a teacher and a writer. Writing is just as much a part of the give and take of human life as speech. Perhaps in the days when Hammurabi's code was pressed, cuneiform by cuneiform, into the wet clay, the written word had greater finality, but in the age of correcting typewriters and word processing, the written word becomes ever more like life—a work-in-progress.

Chapter Two

Revision as a Natural Process

When revision is working best, it is as experimental and exhilarating as learning to walk and talk. One day the toddler stands upright for a surprised, balanced instant, then falls on its well-padded behind, laughs at the sensation, clambers up again and adjusts its balance just enough to stay upright half a second longer before being brought down again by gravity. I believe that the revision an adult writer does is on a continuum with the child's teaching itself to walk. Our lives are full of revision, conscious and unconscious. Revision is a form of learning: it pushes us farther into experience, which alters how we perceive the past and prepares us for the future. I don't mean to describe revision as extraordinary; on the contrary, it seems to me one of the most ordinary of human activities.

For example, one evening shortly after my son Joel turned six, he said, "Thank you for dedicating my dinner to me last night, Mommy," and then after a brief pause added, "What does *dedicate* mean?" He was playing with a new word by trying it out first, then getting feedback from his own ear. When it didn't sound quite right, he consulted his primary reference work, his mother, for further information. He wasn't writing, but he was revising. Similarly, I revised my vocabulary even as I was working on this book. I learned new words: when I was going over chapter one, I had to look up the word *tessellation* because one of the high school students used it in an example I was putting in this book.

This chapter is mostly about revision with children, but it also suggests that the kind of revision young children do can be used by older writers. A child's strategies of playfulness with language and experience can almost always be profitably imitated by older writers.

Certain excellent classroom approaches to language arts such as Whole Language and the Writing Process attempt to create an atmosphere in school where revision is part of the whole project of mastering language. Students read and respond in writing, draft and publish, then read one another's writings. They read complete books rather than excerpts or limited vocabulary readers, and they write in many different circumstances. This is, it seems to me, a great advance over the old theory that you have to perfect spelling and grammar through workbook exercises before you are allowed to write sentences, let alone paragraphs. At the elementary school I attended, we did not write at all. We practiced penmanship, spelling, and grammar, but we never composed anything. For me, unlike the children I see in many schools today, the important reading and writing happened outside of school. I made my own stapled and illustrated books; I wrote the way a child learns to talk, by imitating something that caught my attention. I wanted to get closer to the experience of looking at the funny papers, so I made my own comics, just as a two-year-old sees trucks and makes motor noises while shoving sand around the sand pile. It is the quintessential reaction of children to the world: I encounter it, I play with it (if I'm allowed to), I recreate and imitate it in further play and thus make it mine. Perhaps only in the arts and sports are adults still close to this paradise of play, and I would submit that revision, done in the best way, can be a kind of play too, for children and adults.

When I was first writing those comics and books, I did *not* revise. I wasn't interested in disturbing my stories; I was pretty pleased with them as they were. They had satisfyingly conventional plots from storybooks and the media, and they fulfilled whatever psychological dramas I needed to play out. Only gradually did I learn about deep revision, the large middle ground between the initial plunge and the final polishing. As a child, when I had worked as much as I wanted on a given piece, I simply laid it aside and went on to something else. This can be viewed as one form of revision, particularly suited to very young writers: when you've gone as long as you can, you stop, and start something else afresh.

I remember in second grade reading over what I had written the previous year:

Fredy is a cowboy
Fredy eats beans

Fredy is a cowboy
Becaus his teth gleamz[1]

I had no interest in revising "Fredy," but my new writing had a relationship to what had gone before. In the second grade I wrote stories rather than poems, and they were longer, in script, and had more models from literature because I was reading more books from the library. I was making constant starts, trials, experiments, and the revision was centered not on any particular text, but on my whole relationship to literature. The old saws may be rusty: *If it's worth doing, it's worth doing well.* What if it's not worth doing but it takes doing it for a while to find out? Who's to say what doing well is? Sometimes we polish highly, sometimes we simply check for the most egregious spelling errors and send it off. *Don't start something you can't finish.* Why not start something to see if you want to finish it? What is finishing anyhow? For a six- or seven-year-old, finished is when you're done with it.

For an adult writer too, there are times when the initial flash of insight or inspiration will be enough. Or perhaps a piece is best left as a fragment. Coleridge's "Kubla Khan" exists as a fragment of a dream he could not fully recapture. Or, you actually might hit it right the first time. We need to have different revising strategies, depending on the task or inspiration at hand. There are many adult writers who, like children, do not revise—at least not on paper—or who revise very little. Ironically, I consider it a form of self-discipline *not* to revise certain things I write: that is, I am so accustomed to long bouts of polishing that it's difficult for me to figure out when to stop making changes. At the same time, elementary school children *can* begin to learn to go back and *see again.*

Recently I visited a first grade classroom in a school district that has embraced the Whole Language method of teaching language arts. This was a special treat for me, to be observing instead of doing workshops, and because it was my son's classroom. Joel frequently praised his teacher, Sandra Prince, for never raising her voice. ("Not even when she's mad, Mommy! She never EVER yells at us!") What particularly intrigued me was that Mrs. Prince, an experienced teacher but a relative newcomer to the techniques of Whole Language, had found that the techniques led to a definite improvement

---

[1] Meredith Sue Willis, unpublished manuscript!

in her first graders' reading and writing. The main thing I noticed as I entered the classroom was that it was a place where you were immersed in words and numbers. There were large sheets of paper with word lists hung from hangers, alphabets taped to desks, books stacked on the radiators, Big Books (the large print versions of popular books) propped on an easel, large reports on science experiments, "Math Messages" on the board (which the kids write in a math notebook), and a jar of M&M's for estimating numbers.

I also noticed that these six-year-olds had come to work. They hung up their coats, went to their desks, took out their journals, and started to write. They knew that this is what you do each morning. I was astounded. Even before the Pledge of Allegiance? The room was not silent—there were a few whispers, even a giggle or two—but mostly there was only the scratching of pencils on paper. Some of the students were not writing, but drawing. Mrs. Prince told me that one of the things she likes about this method is that there is no pressure on all the children to work at the same level. Some of the kids have notebooks full of two-page-long entries; others have one word and a drawing. Later I leafed back through Joel's journal and could see how the September entries had been one-word explanations of pictures, but the January pages were almost all writing.

The children worked mostly in blocks of four desks. No one was isolated, and there were lots of interactions among the children, particularly during the next activity, when they were working on writing projects different from the journals. Asking one another for spellings or help with drawing a cat's whiskers was an honored strategy.

While the kids were writing, two mothers arrived, the volunteer "publishers." They were learning to use the classroom computer in order to produce a book for each student. Mrs. Prince took one group of four to the front rug where they were choosing which of their books to publish (not everything gets revised and polished). After the students chose, she worked with them one-on-one. It was at this point, she told me, that she worked hardest on spelling and punctuation, although she also presented occasional five-minute "mini-lessons" of more traditional instruction on, say, punctuation. One of the publishers' jobs is to correct spelling on the computer, but Mrs. Prince pointed out that the student always keeps the original book, and reads it aloud—first to her, so that any words stumbled over and unreadable to the student can be changed before reading it to the publishers. In some cases, when particularly excellent illustrations had been done in the original book, they are clipped and pasted into the published book.

Meanwhile, because of Mrs. Prince's smooth classroom management, the other students continued to work at their desks, some getting new blank books, some illustrating, some going up to the spelling lists and dictionaries for words. They talked at will—mostly about their pieces, getting ideas and responses. Joel complained that he didn't know how to make his Spiderman figure look strong (the book is *Aventchrs of Spitrman: Chapter 1 The Dark Hol*), and Kieran offered to let Joel look at the muscles on his drawing.

Of course, since this is the real world, everything does not advance ideally. The publishers were having technical difficulties. They thought Ryan's book from yesterday had been saved to disk, but it had not. Ryan, a dramatic personality, banged his forehead (not too forcefully) on his desk and said, "Why me? Why me?" He cheered up when he found out that he would have to read his book aloud to the publishers again.

Meanwhile, Mrs. Prince was talking with Pam about her book. Pam, fairly advanced in her skills, paused in reading aloud to note that she wrote "oll" for "all," so she corrected that. At this stage, Mrs. Prince said, a child like Pam is pretty much correcting her own spelling, so Mrs. Prince focused on punctuation: "What could you put here, at the end of the sentence that states something?"

"A period," said Pam, who already knew about punctuation from her own reading and from the five-minute mini-lessons.

Then there was a word Pam couldn't recognize and couldn't remember what she meant, so she said she wanted to do that page over, and Mrs. Prince provided her with more paper, first making sure the pages were numbered and could be reassembled. Mrs. Prince says that an important part of her own role is to keep notes about what the kids are up to on any given day. She will, for example, note that one boy is still illustrating, and if he doesn't get to writing words sometime in the next week or so, she'll encourage him to try.

Mrs. Prince was able to use the principle that everything written does not have to be corrected: the children were learning to separate their drafting from their finished work. They worked at their own speeds. They learned that some final copyediting can be done by another (the "publishers"), although their editor (the teacher) had already encouraged them to add and change, in individual conferences in which she never forgot to praise what she liked.

There were several different kinds of revision going on in Mrs. Prince's first grade classroom. Some pieces were left uncorrected or abandoned altogether; there was interpersonal revision, both informal peer conferencing as the children gave each other ideas, and teacher-student conferencing. I also saw children beginning to do the more sophisticated kinds of revision that I discuss later in this book. I saw them changing media—drawing their ideas, then writing about what they drew. I saw them going back and making changes on their own as they looped back and read over yesterday's writing. This was a classroom with a commitment to maximizing children's chances to learn, and the kind of revision these children were learning seemed to me eminently practical and in tune with their abilities.

The Writing Process and the Whole Language program downplay writing games and exercises in favor of this kind of holistic approach based on classroom organization, but when I am working as a writer-in-the-school, I often use exercises that attempt to create some of the same effects quickly. For the very youngest students, I often use a technique that creates a rough draft through eyes-closed visualization. The actual writing down of the ideas becomes a separate process, a second draft. The exercise here is similar to the one described in chapter one:

TRY THIS: Close your eyes and get very relaxed. It helps to do this if you don't have your legs or arms crossed. Have every part of your body relaxed. Now imagine you are in a real place where you have been. It can be indoors, outdoors, a restaurant, maybe the place you like to go in the summer, a special park, the beach, the mountains, your house of worship, your grandmother's kitchen. Imagine what you smell, what you hear, what you touch. Explore the place, smelling anything you want to, listening, looking, seeing how it feels.

Everyone then takes a breath and comes back from this little vacation. Rather than to take turns talking about what they experienced there, however, I ask the children to write.

TRY THIS: Write as much as you remember of that place—try to include how it looked, how it sounded, smelled, felt, and even tasted.

Especially for the beginning writer, this kind of visualizing, in which an adult walks the child through a remembered place, will result in more details. The memory is immediate in time and imagination, and there is no problem of What Shall I Write About, because the thing has just been experienced.

> I hear the howl
> of the owl in the
> night. I feel the black
> owls soft fethrs. I
> smell the snowe air
> of the cold. I
> loved seeing the
> owls taste of
> love to me.
> the end!
>
> —*Janine, first grade*

TRY THIS: Ask everyone to go back and add one thing: a smell, another sound, another thing seen, the color of something.

> I hear the *black* howl
> of the *black* owl in the
> night. I feel the black
> owls soft fethrs. I
> smell the snowe air
> of the cold. I
> loved seeing the
> owls taste of
> love to me.
> the end!
>
> —*Janine, first grade*

TRY THIS: A super-quick exercise for changing writing is the Boring Cat Game. Everyone gets a sheet of paper and in the middle of the paper writes the word *cat.* The game is to do anything you want to make that interesting—write a story for the cat, a poem, a picture, decorate the letters, etc. You might also try *box* or any other dull word that suits your fancy.

TRY THIS: Another of my favorite writing exercises for first and second graders is a version of the Outside/Inside exercise in chapter one. You take a large sheet of paper (fairly stiff art paper is nice) and make a large circle, which becomes a mask. It can be simple or elaborate, a person or animal or monster. In a sense, the child is creating a first draft of a character by drawing. Turn the paper over, and make the circle again, and this time, within the circle, write the thoughts of the face.

> I am laughing because something funny happind. It was funny because my Mommy said she is having a Bab. And I am laughing.
>
> — *Rosie, first grade*

TRY THIS: Try these alternate flip sides for the mask-character by writing the character description as:

- a poem about the character
- a typical day in the character's life.

TRY THIS: Some other things to do with your character are: write about its house; its dream; its favorite food and a recipe for how to cook it; where it goes, and what it takes with it. Also, have a conversation between two characters: do this in pairs, writing what the characters say, and acting it out.

TRY THIS: After writing, do another version of the same face in a different mood: if your monster was fierce, make it smile. If the girl was laughing, make her angry. Then write on the back what the character is thinking, or why it changed.

TRY THIS: Take the character you have created to a place, using your senses as in the exercise above.

> My crktr (character) went to the
> bsh (beach) she smell food.
> She sees dollfins she
> hears the ocean she
> feels the saed. she taste
> the food.
>
> —*Julie, first grade*

TRY THIS: Have your character have an adventure in that place.

TRY THIS: Make up a group adventure for all of the class in that place.

> At the park there are kids on slides, monkey bars, and swings. The kids in the sand box feel sand. It makes their hands feel yucky.
> The grown-ups are at the lake fishing, or playing golf, or jogging and listening to Walkmans, or sitting at benches and tables watching the kids.
> They hear the kids. They see blue birds. It is a sunny day with flowers. It smells beautiful. You can smell the fresh air.
> "This is fun," say the grown-ups.
> "Exciting! Wow!" say the kids.
> Suddenly it gets cloudy. There is rain, then snow, hail, fog, thunder and lightning, a storm, a hurricane, a tornado.
> "Let's go home," say the grown-ups.
> "No!" say the kids. "Let's stay longer!"
> "Be quiet!"
> "You be quiet!"
>
> *—Ms. Milunic's first grade class*
> *Walnut Avenue School, Cranford, New Jersey*

This description was done by the students (and teacher) calling out sentences and then discussing among themselves what should happen next. I wrote their sentences on the board, making a great show of occasionally making a mistake, or writing down one idea and then taking another idea and scratching out the first one. On my next visit, I brought in the story typed, and the class acted it out—everyone sitting at his or her seat and being buffeted by the tornado, cheering on cue. I then read, sentence by sentence, what we had written *and acted* and the group made the changes and additions (in italics below) in the next draft. Many of the changes came from things that happened in the acting out. Then we continued and finished the story as a group. The children's changes were mostly one-word improvements or corrections, usually of a phrase that didn't seem right to them.

> At the park there are kids on slides, monkey bars, and swings. The kids in the sand box feel sand. It makes their hands feel *gooey*.

The grown-ups are at the lake fishing, or playing golf, or jogging and listening to *their earphones,* or sitting at benches and tables watching the kids.

They hear the kids. They see blue birds. It is a sunny day with flowers. It smells beautiful. You can smell the fresh air.

"This is fun," say the grown-ups.

"Exciting! Wow!" say the kids.

Suddenly it gets cloudy. There is rain, then snow, hail, fog, thunder and lighting, a storm, a hurricane, a tornado.

"Let's go home," say the grown-ups.

"No!" say the kids. "Let's stay longer! *This is Bogus!*"

"Be quiet!"

"You be quiet!"

"The tornado will blow you away!"

"Okay, we'll go home."

Then the weather changed again.

Kelly said, "Look! It stopped! Let's go back and play."

"Okay!" They all cheer.

Young children learn the process of revision piecemeal, of course, but I want to emphasize empowering children by teaching them the pleasure of manipulating words, memories, and imagination.

* * * * *

As students get older, revision can also be presented to them as an activity done by professional and creative writers. The idea of writing as a profession didn't occur to me until I was well into my teens. I had no models of adult writers; I certainly knew nothing of the business and industry of book publishing and selling. But I did begin to recognize certain writers' names and to associate power with their invocation: Shakespeare! Tolstoy-and-Dostoevsky! Margaret Mitchell! I read articles about writers, and even began to play at being a writer myself. One summer, having read in *Reader's Digest* that great writers spend an hour a day or more (!) at their desks, I committed myself to being at the typewriter one hour each morning, rain or shine. I remember, one extremely hot summer morning, sitting on the rough home-poured concrete of our little patio with my mother's old black Underwood typewriter on a stool in front of me. How could anyone really do this? I thought. An hour is so long! It's so hot. I'm not cut out for this.

Then I learned that Great Authors revise over and over again. With a new self-awareness, I began to look at the stories and personal essays and poems I had been writing for my own entertainment. I found that making word choices was actually fun. Crimson? Scarlet? Incarnadine? I imagined the Great Author in a room lined with bookshelves, with one large powerful hand clutching his hair while the other fingered his words as if they were old coins. He held them to the light as if candling eggs, he sniffed them as if they were little vials of perfume. I saw him in my mind, and simultaneously I saw myself in my attic room at my small student desk. I saw myself as from a distance, and tried to revise myself into this revising Great Author. I didn't look like him, but I tried at least to do what I imagined he did: I looked at my story word by word. I had written: "I was insulted that he thought no more of my power." I scratched out the word *power* so that the sentence read: "I was insulted that he thought no more of my *abilities.*" A page later, I had written: "Then in spite of everything, I slept." I changed it to: "*Finally* in spite of everything, *I did sleep.*"

Were the changes an improvement? It depends on how you look at it. I cannot say they are the changes I would make today. "Did sleep" seems fussy, as if I wanted to make the tone of my story more genteel or to show off my knowledge of complex past tenses. If I had been that fourteen-year-old girl's teacher, I would probably have been pleased mostly by the sheer bulk and ambition of the forty-page story. I might have felt duty-bound to point out that "in spite of everything" is a phrase that needs to be set off by commas at both ends. But I think I would have appreciated the experiment in tone that is represented by "finally" and "did sleep." When I scratched out "that" and replaced it with "the" or changed "lice or fleas" to "some horrible parasite," I was teaching myself that words are malleable.

Should a teacher or reader faced with such a student writer suggest that "lice or fleas" is more concrete and thus more vivid than "some horrible parasite?" My instinct is not to intervene too much with anyone who is—for himself or herself—playing with words. I would rather give models of the best literature and trust the student to discover the power of plain, concrete speech later, although over against this is my belief that any respectful response, no matter how detailed or strong, is useful to a young writer. Writing is not, after all, a sacred ritual that can be done only one way without angering the gods. Nor are young writers such frail beings that they cannot bear some contradictions and varying opinions. The most important thing, it seems to me, is a sense of respect on the part of the teacher-editor for the student's own ideas and projects—and it's sometimes difficult to learn to participate in the younger writer's process of writing without taking it over. But this sense of respect is vital to the art of teaching.

TRY THIS: Look for a piece of writing you did long ago: a story or poem from adolescence or childhood would be ideal. Don't mark on it, but make a copy and read it over. Edit it as best you can. Type it up. How does it seem, turned into a piece of adult writing? Something publishable as children's literature? Has it lost any of its flavor? Are the two pieces simply too different to compare?

TRY THIS: After reading the old piece, lay it aside, and write a new version of the same material. Ask yourself the same questions as above. Is there anything in either of these versions that you could use now for more than an exercise?

TRY THIS: Try out either the polished or redrafted piece on a person of the same age as you were when you wrote the original. What does the child or young adult think of it? Are they just being polite?

TRY THIS: To use this exercise with children, have them bring in a composition or story from some previous year and make a new version or revision.

TRY THIS: Exchange papers among students, and revise someone else's old piece. Remember to use copies of these things, as the originals may be precious to someone someday.

TRY THIS: Give the student a copy of the teacher's (or other adult's) piece of writing to revise.

TRY THIS: Give out copies of something you wrote long ago that doesn't have an ending, and ask everyone to try finishing it.

PART TWO

◆

GOING DEEPER

Chapter Three

Learning to Revise by Editing Other People's Writing

During my college years, I learned more about how literature works from my creative writing classes than from my literature classes. My literature classes tended to create a hushed atmosphere around the great works. We admired and interpreted, always assuming the most profound intentions behind every word choice, every iota of punctuation. In the creative writing classes, however, we were dealing with unfinished works: not bad or failed literature, but literature-in-progress. We tinkered with one another's writings, pounded at them and stretched them, taught ourselves and each other about the malleability of the written word and why people write in the first place.

Learning how to revise by looking at someone else's work is one of the reasons so many writers search out peer groups. In a peer group, you not only get responses to your own writing, you also learn by seeing someone else's work developing, by hearing about someone else's struggles, challenges, and plans. We are wrong to think of writing as an activity done only in solitude. Much of it is, but always with the echoes of previously written words in our ears, and always with at least a vague image of a potential reader.

One assignment I have used with adults and children for many years is simply to revise a piece of student writing. If you are a teacher, you may have a favorite piece of your own. Often I use the example below; it seems to raise a lot of interesting questions and inspire creative effort in many different students. I have continued to use it because of its brevity and the way it brings up issues of revision and how to teach writing. It was written by a junior high school student in a neighborhood in Brooklyn that had many empty, overgrown lots and blocks of dilapidated tenements, as well as a handful of highrise projects. The original assignment was simple:

TRY THIS: Describe as vividly as possible a real person you have met or seen but don't know too well: that is, not your mother or your brother, but someone you see in your neighborhood or on your block.

A seventh grader named Regina wrote:

The Bummy Old Lady

She was very old and had bummy clothes and she had long hanging lips. She drinks a lot of wine and begs and also she doesn't have any shoes. She has no house, no kids, not even a husband. Her clothes do not match, and also her clothes have a lot of holes. She has on a man's pants with holes in them and also she is very dirty, and she has an overcoat with holes in it and she begs and begs and begs. And plus she has brown eyes, a big long nose, a man's voice, a scarred-up face, no hair and green teeth.

In my first book on writing, *Personal Fiction Writing,* I wrote of this piece: "I have always liked this description—particularly its rhythms of repetition—although I feel strongly that the last sentence is out of place."[1] In other words, it was a piece that seemed to me to have merit, but also some clear problems that could be picked out easily even by young students. For example, most children notice that the last sentence is an afterthought. They pick out places where usage could be standardized. For adults, the piece raises some questions about style and even educational priorities: is the repetition a stylistic advantage or a fault? What about beginning a sentence with *and*? Is it ever acceptable to shift tenses in the middle of a paragraph?

The basic revision assignment I do with this piece is as follows:

TRY THIS: Read "The Bummy Old Lady" and change it to make it better. Add to it, move things around, take things away, change words. Do anything you want to make it better.

Some students will make only stylistic changes such as getting rid of repetitions or adding specific details. Others want to know if they

---

[1] Meredith Sue Willis, *Personal Fiction Writing* (New York: Teachers & Writers Collaborative, 1984), p. 184.

can really do *anything*, and, when faced with that open-ended proposition, will actually rewrite the whole piece, re-envision it, sometimes even give it a happy ending.

I was amazed some years ago when a class of fourth graders were selecting which of their own pieces to put in an anthology, and a number of them chose their revisions of "The Bummy Old Lady." Did they get a special sense of empowerment from working on someone else's writing? Did they find it easier to look at another person's drafts? A girl at P.S. 87 in Manhattan wrote:

> This woman is just like a mouse with no hole because when she gets money, all she does is buy drugs and take them. She wears the same old holey clothes every day. She doesn't have a house or kids. Nobody likes her because all she does is beg. This lady is also very ugly. She has brown eyes, an ugly scarred-up face, a big, long, doofy nose, a man's voice—baldheaded, big dragon long lips, and green teeth from drinking so much. All she does is talk and beg, beg and talk, talk and beg.
>
> —*Ashaki Rucker, fourth grade*

Ashaki grouped similar details together, and she replaced the tacked-on ending. She retained the repetition, but used her own words and reorganized the piece so that the ending is stronger.

Some older students, eighth graders at Bragaw Avenue School in Newark, New Jersey, first had a class discussion that touched on grammar, consistent tenses, and organization. Then two girls wrote the following versions:

> Miss Johnson, she is old and has bummy clothes. She wears a pair of man's pants with holes in them and a holey overcoat with it that doesn't match. She has long hanging lips, brown eyes, a big nose, no hair, a scarred up face, and when she talks to beg for food in a man's tone you can see her green teeth in her mouth.
>
> She has no house, no job, no kids, not even a high school education, or a husband. She is very dirty and smelly too. She has nowhere to run or even to hide. This poor old woman is forced to live outside.
>
> She drinks wine and beer to take away her worries and fears. Although it helps her when the bottle is tilted upside down, it all comes back to her when she puts it down.
>
> —*Jacqueline T. Britt, eighth grade*

*   *   *   *   *

Sally used to drink lots of wine and begged for money. She was very old
and had bummy clothes and no shoes. She had long hanging lips and
big brown eyes, a big nose, a man's voice and a scarred up face, and
no hair and yellow teeth. She had no house, kids, and husband. She
used to tell me that when she was young she was very beautiful & had
lots of friends and money. Sally said one day she met this handsome
man named Bob & fell in love but little did she know he only wanted
her money. She asked him to marry her, but he would never say anything. Sally never kept money in the bank, it was always in her house.
One day when she came home from work, all her money and valuable
things were gone. When she saw this, she started drinking. Sally started
drinking so much that she lost her job and house. Sally is dead now but
I still remember her scarred-up face and clothes.

—*Zakina McDaniel, eighth grade*

I especially like the way these girls give the bummy old lady a
name and a history. Zakina even puts herself into the piece as a re-
ceiver of Sally's story: "She used to tell me," and "Sally is dead now
but I still remember." There was no alienation from the bummy old
lady: Jacqueline and Zakina saw her as a real woman with real mis-
fortunes, a story worth telling and retelling.

TRY THIS: As an alternative to "The Bummy Old Lady," I
made up this story for very young students:

A Boring Story

We had a very very very very very very very very nice dogg. It did
something to help us once.
Oh, by the way, it was a black dogg.

TRY THIS: For another alternative to "The Bummy Old
Lady," here is the beginning of a play, *David and Maria*, written by
junior high students in the South Bronx.

David and Maria

A crowded hallway in the school. Students screaming and running back and forth.

CAST:

MARIA . . . a girl with light skin, medium size, black hair, a nice smile,
and a switch to her walk. She is shy, and when she gets around her
boyfriend, she always stutters. She wears tight pants.

DAVID . . . tall with black hair, dark brown eyes, and dimples when he smiles.

MR. MILLER . . . an old-fashioned mean teacher with a potbelly.

VARIOUS VOICES OF STUDENTS: Did you hear what happened to me today? Are we going to play football tomorrow? Did you know what Richard said?

DAVID (*in a voice trying to get over the crowd*): Hey, Maria! Come over here!

MARIA: What is it, Davey?

(*They go dashing through the crowd, trying to get to each other.*)

DAVID: Meet you after school under the train station?

MARIA: Okay, sugarplum.

(*Then he takes her by the hand to a corner where nobody is. He looks at her lips and she looks at his. Slowly they come together.*)

(*Suddenly Mr. Miller taps David on the shoulder.*)

MR. MILLER (*clearing his throat*): Don't you think you two should be getting upstairs now? David, I'll speak to you after class.

(*David and Maria give each other a look.*)

I tried a variation of "The Bummy Old Lady" assignment with a class of undergraduates at Cooper Union. Some of the students had done some teaching themselves, and all of them had a lot of ideas about what makes for good teaching. Again I used "The Bummy Old Lady," but this time I asked students to write down what they would say to Regina.

TRY THIS: Pretend to be the teacher of Regina, the seventh grade girl who wrote "The Bummy Old Lady." How would you react to this paper? How would you suggest that she rewrite it? As you made your suggestions to her, what would be your priorities? What would you focus on first?

Reactions were various, some less than serious. Scott Rees, for example, wrote an imaginary dialogue between himself and Regina:

"No, get out of here!"
"Yup, it's true, and also she can hardly walk."

"I don't believe a word of it."
"It's not made up."
"Well, I certainly hope not!"
"You're silly."
"How true."

Other students made lots of circles and arrows and notes and took a more serious tone:

You have to decide about which tense you want to use. . . . Perhaps if you group the physical descriptions together and then what she does and what she has, it will make your piece seem more fluid.

—*Dianne Karonkiewicz*

* * * * *

Tell more about her lips and how she speaks with them. What does it look like to speak with hanging lips? What does she beg for? Money, food, mercy?

—*Carolyn Gatto*

* * * * *

It's interesting how you relate her to men: not having a husband or children, but wearing men's clothes and looking like a man. There might be something here to elaborate on if you choose.

—*Laurie Pearsall*

* * * * *

You should consider making a poem of this because the imagery was brilliant.

—*Bryan Crockett*

* * * * *

Don't sell your soul. GREAT WORK!!! Check out the first chapter of James Joyce's *Portrait of the Artist.* He tries to describe people with the same language but fails.

—*Tristan Spill*

The exercise led to a lengthy discussion about what matters most in teaching the creative arts. Some of the students felt Regina's piece was a sacred expression of her personality, her literary innocence. Others felt that you can't let the jarring shifts in tense and the overuse of "and" and "also" go uncorrected. This led us to debate the necessity of preparing a student for the work world—the "real" world—with the ability to write "correctly." "Then," said one student, "all you're doing is turning self-expression and art into a tool for making a living!"

"Yeah, right," said someone else. "Exactly. We have to make a living, and the question is, does our education prepare us to make a living?"

"But isn't art different? Isn't art something more than making a living?"

"And," I added, just to make sure no bases were left uncovered, "what about the student's self-esteem? What if emphasizing the good parts of this piece gives her the confidence to go into her regular grammar class and do better than she ever did before?" (I found myself having visions of the girl's life being changed: she goes on to become a lawyer, a Supreme Court justice, all because her writing teacher commented favorably on her use of repetition in her descriptive essay!)

The students went on to discuss their own strenuous year of what are called "foundation" art courses at Cooper Union: whether or not their creativity was squelched by having to do exercises. "Well," said one student, Peter Mullaney, "I taught an art class in a high school once and I had them do a still life drawing of a stapler. Just a regular old stapler. I asked them to make it as realistic as possible. And this one kid did a sort of graffiti-style stapler that was so much more interesting to look at than the realistic ones, but I had to say to him, 'Yes, it *is* more interesting, but what about the assignment? What about mastering drawing?'"

The win-win answer is that students need all of the above: to know the value of being critiqued and edited, to master strategies for using writing in practical situations, and also to preserve what is unique, special, expressive, and creative in their work.

Even younger students have their opinions on the best ways to teach. At the end of my Expository Writing Tutorial by Mail course, I gave the following assignment:

TRY THIS: I'd like you to pretend you've been invited to speak to a group of teachers. You are still yourself, a student, but everyone agrees you are a model writing student with excellent ideas, and the teachers have chosen you to tell what worked best for you over the years in improving your writing. The teachers are eager to hear your point of view. Try to tell them what has helped and hindered your writing, both creative and expository.

Some of the students wrote a standard essay, but others responded imaginatively to the idea of making an address to a captive audience of teachers. Jen Colaguori wrote:

A Speech

Good afternoon. It's a real privilege for me to be here today. I enjoy writing so much, that when I was asked to come here, I was overjoyed to be able to share my ideas and opinions with you. In my early years of elementary school, the teachers stressed the use of creativity in my writing. When we wrote, they didn't correct the grammar or spelling, because they thought that this would lead us away from creativity. This, I find, to be the key ingredient to a good piece of writing. Once I reached third grade, or thereabouts, my teacher introduced us to the use of adjectives and adverbs for description. This is the first time I actually dealt with grammar. I think it is very important to create the scene for your readers and give them as much detail as possible without overdoing it. I just recently had an assignment to write an essay describing myself. This was a great way to get a feeling for adjectives. I set up the essay as if I were looking in a mirror. I first described what I saw, and then I described the things that you wouldn't know about a person by just looking in a mirror.

When I started middle school all of my language arts teachers taught similes and metaphors. They are perfect ways to create scenes without using too many adjectives. We had to write stories using at least three examples of similes or metaphors, and then we compared them to stories we had written before without them. They can really make the difference in a descriptive piece.

When I started the Johns Hopkins program, it seemed that what they stressed most was to grab your readers at the beginning and hold on to them until the end. My tutor gave me a few ideas of how to catch the reader from the beginning. For example, start off your essay with a question. This will make your reader keep reading to find out what your opinion is on the subject. Or, you could start with a quotation or something funny about the subject. She also told me not to sum everything up in a concluding paragraph, because this seems to lose the interest of the reader and therefore, make your piece come to a downfall.

My parents always told me I had a talent for writing. They encouraged me to use descriptive words, too. Over the years I found that using dialogue in my pieces was an easy way to catch the reader from the beginning. I also found that keeping a diary gave me an understanding of things that really happen in life.

This year our language arts class wrote plays, and entered them in the New Jersey Young Playwrights Festival. Although I didn't win, I did get very useful information from the readers. They said that I set up my characters very well, even though there were a lot of characters that were not needed in telling the story. (Which is another key point to make sure you cover when you are writing.) But, I should concentrate more on what was needed in the story, and not to stray from the subject.

Over the years, I think I have absorbed many useful hints in writing, and I am very proud to be able to pass them on to you.

Thank you.

I have to think that Jen has indeed "absorbed many useful hints" during her school years (and it was fun for me to see her telling back what she had picked up from our tutorial—perhaps not precisely what I had thought were the most important things). It is worth noting what this thirteen-year-old sees as important: her parents' encouragement, of course, and that of other adults—she *expects* praise and support from teachers. Notice that she recommends introducing grammatical and structural concepts in a way that makes them useful: she wants to write vivid pieces that affect other people. Also, she likes her teachers to submit student work to contests and events in the world outside the school, adding a sense of breadth and importance to the writing.

Other students made other points. One high school junior offered a harsh critique of the way writing is taught in his academically rigorous private school:

Writing is fun. Work is not. Writing and work are mutually exclusive: good writing can not be born of a laborious effort. Many teachers assign voluminous amounts of writing hoping that some small bit of good writing will be created. This is a horrible approach. This will only make students turn their backs on writing and walk away with a bitter taste in their mouths. Teachers in general do many things which I have found to be wrong with regards to correcting student writing. It seems that many teachers start by giving a paper an A+ and then begin subtracting points for every error. Using this method, the student is only allowed to see the bad points of his writing, which are usually circled in red. When he corrects these errors, he will almost always end up with a mediocre paper with few grammatical errors and even fewer traces of original thought or well developed ideas. Instead, teachers should start out thinking of a paper as an F and then circle every *good* point in it, thus allowing a student to see that he did a certain thing well. In every piece of writing, there are bound to be some noteworthy points. Instead of correcting grammar, the student is free to develop his good points and thereby have a stronger paper overall. By correcting a paper in a negative way, as most teachers, like it or not, do, the student is forced to conform to a simplistic and confining style in which he can not find any style of his own. The student will be discouraged, only seeing the bad points of his writing and he will then get the impression that his writing as a whole is bad.

In most cases, it is the teacher, and not the student who is wrong. Sure, many students have grammatical errors which need fixing, and the teacher can note these things, but the teacher should never say a negative thing without mentioning something positive. Instead of saying, "Your paper has many careless grammatical mistakes," say "While your paper contains misuses of the language, I feel that you raise some interesting points and original ideas." One way, the student sees himself as a poor writer, the other, he sees himself as someone who made mistakes, but has potential. . . . Open-ended essay assignments are the best: "Write an essay about a time when you learned a lesson," a teacher should say. The students will be forced to actually *think* about this and be creative in developing an idea. When a teacher says, "Write an eight-page paper on abortion and make sure it follows the format outlined on this paper," all he will get are groans from every student as well as unimaginative and worthless papers. Creative writing is *the* most important ingredient to any writing course.

I know it is a radical idea, students actually thinking and using their imaginations, but I fear that if this method is not utilized, as a student deletes his grammatical mistakes, so too will he delete his unused, undeveloped imagination. Imagination is like a car's engine. If it is not used, it will soon rust away and disappear, leaving only a shell behind, but if it is constantly run and checked and properly harnessed, it can be a wonderful tool. Too often have I seen students with no imagination left. Imagination that was circled with a red pen and soon deleted, because it did not fit the format. These tight restrictions and insipid rules have all but eliminated the truly creative writing process for many students. . . .

English teachers have a special responsibility. Unlike math and history teachers, these educators are entrusted with a child's imagination, one of their greatest gifts. What a great tragedy it is to see these young minds forced to conform to a teacher's rigid structure, for as they conform, they gain a grade, but lose their identities. Of course, some lucky ones may buck the system and sustain their imaginations, as I have, but more often than not, these students give up and turn writing into a chore just for a grade, and as they do, their imaginations silently wither away into space, and this is a greater tragedy than anyone could ever write, for when imagination is finally snuffed out, so is the human race.

I believe I have made my point abundantly clear. What makes for good writing is creativity and imagination, not structural detail and grammatical perfection. Make assignments fun and open ended, allowing a student to add *his* unique personality to his writing. Do not suck the life from a paper with a red pen as you would suck the meat from a crab leg. What makes a piece of writing different is what makes it great. Writing should not be a chore. Writing is fun.

—*Billy Maris, eleventh grade*

After a peroration like that one, it's hard to go back to offering little exercises that might help improve writing by small increments. But Billy Maris is hardly the first person, nor will he be the last, to be bitter over papers covered with red-ink slashes. Especially when the red-inked work is the final product, students have no recourse. Student papers, however faulty, do not deserve such treatment.

This is another reason that these exercises involving looking at someone else's writing are so important: they put the students, not just the teacher, in positions of power. The trick is not merely to let the oppressed be the oppressors for a while, but rather to suggest a new way of looking at another person's work. When you revise someone else's work, actually involving yourself in it, you are in a position of power, but you need to use that power to understand how the piece works from the inside out, and how it can be made better.

This is what the great editors and teachers do. They make a piece their own, not by changing it so much that the original writer's work is lost, but by undergoing a process of transformation that moves them as well as the writer in new directions. Experiencing this process—as an editor or teacher—is one important way to improve your own writing.

TRY THIS: Try pairing older students with younger ones in the lower grades of your school for editing sessions. After the editing sessions, have everyone discuss how it went, what worked and didn't.

TRY THIS: In pairs, try working on one another's writing by changing roles. In each case, don't just act it out, but actually do the editing or revising, taking turns so that both people play all the following roles:

1. Be the worst possible teacher to your partner. Do all the worst things teachers could do to a paper.
2. Do the opposite: be a good teacher.
3. Be a magazine editor considering this work for publication. Don't pay attention to grammar or spelling, just make the piece more interesting to a reader of your magazine.
4. Be a copy editor. Concentrate on spelling, grammar, etc. Your job isn't style, but correctness.

Here are a few more revision exercises using other people's writing or group writing:

TRY THIS: Do a group writing on the blackboard in your class. A good choice would be a portrait of a person or a place. Make typed copies of this group writing and hand them out for the class members to revise individually, then read one another's revisions and try to identify the best strategies for revision.

Here is the group writing of an eighth grade class at Bragaw Avenue School in Newark, New Jersey, along with one student's revision:

Sports Park U.S.A.

Smell of pizza! You also smell wet grass from the misty fountain of the miniature golf. You have the feeling—the mood—of too many choices. You hear loud video games like Street Fighter II. You also hear shots of cannon of the batting cage. Feet moving, people screaming. It looks crowded with games and people and colorful posters.
   Meeting girls/boys
   Prizes—not great—no money.

Sports Park U.S.A.

When you walk in, you can smell pizza. You can also smell the wet grass travelling through the misty fountains of the miniature golf court.

You have the feeling and the mood of spending money. You hear the loud roar of video games like Street Fighter II. You also hear shots from the cannons in the batting cage. You also feel feet moving and people screaming. This one room is crowded with games, people, and colorful posters of people and other exciting games.

Meeting girls/boys is the best part about Sports Park U.S.A. And worst of all, if you don't have money, you can't win prizes and that's not good.

—*Aseelah Williams*

TRY THIS: Make a class collection of ideas for ways to revise. Publish this collection with the school computer and xerox machine. Use the booklets when you are editing each other's pieces or your own. Give copies of the booklet to other classes in your grade and in lower grades.

Unscrambling stories is another enjoyable way to get into revision.

TRY THIS: Type the following two scrambled stories, then cut them out and put them in an envelope. Each person dumps the sentences out on the desk and puts them in the best order.

I.
Ellen and I won.
As Ellen told a story, her voice sounded funny.
The judges looked at you funny.
Next came my turn.
Everyone had their fingers crossed.
Ellen and I got to go to the district contest.
The day of the story telling contest, I was nervous.
It was March 17.

II.
My heart pounding, I took another step.
I said, "I'll never go down there again!"
I put my feet down very carefully and clutched the rail.
I screamed and ran up the stairs as fast as I could.
I didn't want to go down there.
The sound sent a chill up my spine.
The thing squealed!
The light in the basement was broken.
It slithered past me, touching my leg.
My foot landed on something soft and squishy.
I heard a noise like something scurrying.

TRY THIS: Here is a scrambled story for slightly older students. Proceed as above.

> A man was riding on a sleek, black motorbike with a swastika on it.
> He wore black boots with mud caked on the bottom.
> I was walking my dog late one Saturday night when I saw him for the first time.
> He wore a black shiny jacket and a hard hat with a long point on top.
> His low deep voice echoed in my head as he laughed continuously.
> Whenever I see him I think of all the Jews that died in Nazi Germany.
> He was constantly riding up and down on the sidewalk.

Another way of writing better, paradoxically, is to learn what poor writing is by "reverse revision," that is, take something well written, and see how bad you can make it.

TRY THIS: Take some clear or beautiful passage of writing and see how bad you can make it. You can do this in class, emphasizing one problem at a time. Thus, try bad grammar once, or bad spelling (with little kids this is fun, because then you have them exchange papers and correct the spelling). Or, with older and more sophisticated writers, work on being too latinate or too purple. Here is a sentence from Ecclesiastes (in the King James version), followed by George Orwell's well-known "revision":

> I returned, and saw under the sun, that the race is not to the swift, nor the battle to the strong, neither yet bread to the wise, nor yet riches to men of understanding, nor yet favor to men of skill; but time and chance happeneth to them all.

> Objective consideration of contemporary phenomena compels the conclusion that success or failure in competitive activities exhibits no tendency to be commensurate with innate capacity, but that a considerable element of the unpredictable must inevitably be taken into account.

The relationship of editor/teacher and writer/student brings me to the next chapter of this book, which discusses revising your own writing by using other people's responses.

Chapter Four

Learning to Revise by Using Other People's Comments on Your Writing

How do you best use other people to help you go deeper into your own writing? Since revision fundamentally consists of trying to look with new eyes, it follows that one excellent approach is to bring in literally new eyes: other readers. There is nothing more important than the response of a good reader in making the plunge into deep revision. For children, almost any friendly response helps to sustain their interest in the writing project and to stimulate new ideas. The combined efforts of several children or a whole class can push ideas much farther than a single child would go when writing alone—particularly in the younger grades—and such group writings are an ideal way for the teacher to make points and give mini-lessons without interfering in an individual child's work.

This chapter begins with ideas for group revising in elementary school, but keep in mind that these ideas are also good for adults. At my first public reading, I shared the podium with a woman who was an actor as well as a writer. Many of her actor friends were in the audience. For several years I had been working alone, and when I read a section of my novel-in-progress to this audience, I was both stunned and thrilled to hear them laugh. They laughed loudly, leaning forward, and I even saw one man slap his knee. They were demonstrative and appreciative, and while I had known there was some wry humor in my writing, I had never imagined it making other people laugh. This was a great breakthrough for me—I took heart about my future as a writer, and became more aware of myself as a humorist. I also began to read passages of my prose aloud as a revision technique, to test the sound of it.

You can show children the interactive nature of writing through group writing and group revision. I love to model revision with a class through a group poem or story written on the board or on an easel (like the group story in chapter two). A classroom teacher can arrange for the class to work on such a collaborative piece over a period of days by leaving the piece in front of the class, where students can go up and work on it in groups or individually. New ideas can be written in different colors; if the sentences on the easel become crowded, tape on flaps of paper. Rip pages in two and expand their length. All of these techniques are used by professional writers as they come up with new ideas. This is a perfect opportunity to demonstrate the making-mud-pies quality of rough drafting: the objective is to allow oneself the freedom to smoosh around, add, subtract, and generally make a delightful mess.

TRY THIS: Have the group choose the most boring object in the room. Stay away from objects with personality (stuffed animals) or anything with too much color (the ceramic rainbow pencil holder). A standard board-of-education-issue clock is good, or anything flat: the floor, the acoustic tile ceiling, the blackboard.

After choosing the most boring thing, the students close their eyes, put the boring thing in their minds, and observe and explore it imaginatively using their senses. What would it sound like if tapped, taste like if licked? This is already a form of revision: taking the boring thing and mulling it over, reconstituting it imaginatively, expanding a description of it. Part of the point of this exercise, of course, is that anything so explored becomes not boring at all: taste the blackboard? How entertainingly gross!

The group story, then, begins with a dictated description of the boring thing using as many sense details as possible. You can make a point about revising by grouping all the sound details together, the smells, etc.

Next, everyone brainstorms some things that might happen—or even have happened—to the boring thing. Note down three or more ideas of possible story lines. I like to make a Tree of Possibilities on the board—that is, each idea has several more ideas branching off from it. Often the students' ideas will point up different types of fiction. If you wait long enough, you will almost certainly have examples of at least three types of fiction:

1. Total fantasy (the ceiling turns into a monster).

2. Realistic but unlikely (there is a great earthquake and the ceiling buries the adult in charge).

3. Realistic and entirely possible—typical classroom conflicts, serious or humorous, that have actually happened or might happen (someone throws paint at the ceiling and blames another student).

After several possible story ideas are sketched out, you can choose one or more of them, and continue with different possibilities for *that* story line. The variety of ideas enables the leader to keep the class from getting too engrossed in gore, for example, while still allowing the gory ideas to be respected and noted down along with the less gory ones.

Trying new directions and different possibilities, retracing your steps and trying new ways, are all part of how deep revision works. Mrs. Vaccarella's fourth grade class at the Doyle School in Wood-Ridge, New Jersey, dictated the following basic story to me about their fatal blackboard (green these days). We sketched out the collaborative story with its two endings, including the visualization and sketches of other possible ideas, in about fifteen minutes.

Blackboard

It has a lot of writing (homework) on it, and when you're bad, your name is on it. It feels cold, smooth, and dry. When you scrape it with your nail, you get the squeaking sound and you sneeze from the dust.

Continuation #1:

Suddenly it turns into a giant lizard with a furry tail. Whatever it sees, it eats. The kids tried to fight, but they keep sneezing. First it ate the teacher, then Stephen. "Good-bye!" Suddenly the light bulbs turn into poison snakes that kill the monster. Stephen fell out of the monster. Each kid in the class got a snake to take home.

Continuation #2:

The blackboard falls on a girl who is walking by it to write her name on the board. Dominique says, "Get me out of here!"

Nicole says, "Let's help her."

Stephen says, "Leave her there."

The girls start to pick up pieces of blackboard and throw them away, but the boys throw them back.

Finally, Sean says, "Ah, let's go to the movies."

The girls get Dominique out, and she says, "Now let's US go to the movies too."

The exercise could end here or could be developed into a class play. I like the exercise because of its flexibility; the teacher can emphasize whatever he or she chooses: you might work very slowly, changing a word, rejecting a whole story line if it begins to get boring, doing a horror story for Halloween or a humorous story for a class booklet. You can start over, finish a little collection of blackboard stories, ultimately choose one as the authorized version—or not.

TRY THIS: The rest of the assignment is to finish one or more of the story possibilities as a group or individually. The teacher, in order to make sure that all the types of fiction get included, might assign some students to do fantasy, some to do possible-but-unlikely stories, some to do realistic ones. You could, with older students, use specific genres of literature that they might be encountering in their reading: The Mystery of the Old Blackboard; The Blackboard: A Dramatic Monologue; Life of a Blackboard; Ode to a Blackboard; The Blackboard from Outer Space—including an assignment to do a nonfiction version with research on blackboards, an account of some actual incident with the thing, or an interview with other students about it.

In each case, try to keep a descriptive passage as the opening paragraph.

TRY THIS: Go back individually to your favorite version of the group story and write it again, copying the parts you like best, but changing anything you want to. You might, for example, use the names of your friends for the parts that other people had. Go ahead and finish it, however you like. If you have to change the beginning, that's okay too.

TRY THIS: Do some on-the-spot polishing. Count how many senses you used, and add one more. Add a color or a smell or a touch or a shape or a sound—just insert a little arrow or write between the lines. Try adding a metaphor or simile.

TRY THIS: Have a reading to see how the various endings came out.

TRY THIS: Make a play out of one of the stories or a booklet of the best versions of one story.

TRY THIS: After doing this exercise as a class, try it again with a different description. Try it in small groups, in pairs, as individuals.

One student imagined and described his parakeet, then made up a realistic but fictional story:

"Lady"

My pet parakeet named Lady tastes like feathers when you lick her. She feels soft. Lady is green on her belly with white on her head. There are black stripes over the white. When she chirps it sounds sweet.

One day my parakeet flew out of its cage. The door was open to outside. I ran to close it but she was outside already. I ran outside to get her. She flew up, up, up. Luckily she was trained. I called out, Lady! She flew down on my finger. I was very happy. I then put her back in her cage. She didn't fly out for a year so I bought her a playmate. My brother named him Bluebird. That's another story.

—*Jamie Zimak, fourth grade*

TRY THIS: Do the same exercise by having the group choose a place everyone knows. Close your eyes and imagine yourself in a real place, good or bad, indoors or out. It might be a restaurant or a museum or a church or a synagogue or a park or a beach. It might be on the bus or subway. Wherever you put yourself, use your senses in your imagination to observe what you smell and perhaps taste, what you hear, see, and feel—both things you might touch with your hands and the way the place feels to your whole body—its temperature, any breezes that might be passing. Let as many people as possible contribute a detail.

After doing the group writing, ask each student what happens next. Do people come? Is there a storm? Now try this exercise individually. You could do your own room or your grandmother's kitchen or the place you go for vacation.

For children, working with other people is a means of keeping the momentum going, of exploring further, of trying out various ideas—thus of revising more deeply. One child alone, faced with an interesting beginning, may lose the thread by the second day and end up sitting and staring. For such a child, the stimulation of a small group, of other kids saying "Hey, what if—" can be extremely helpful. The solitary artist is a relatively recent model, anyhow, dating mostly from the romantic movement. Many sculptors, for example, are dependent on craftspeople to convert their models to monumental casts of bronze, and one of the twentieth century's most characteristic art forms, film, is a group effort (even when one *auteur* receives most of the credit). Most artists need to seek out community at some point; whether consciously or not, we all collect ideas and revise our work based on the responses of others.

I say this to reemphasize how natural it is for children (and all of us) to work together. A structured way to get responses from other people is what is now called conferencing. Teachers are increasingly aware of the importance of students' working together. Edna Patton, a high school English teacher in West Caldwell, New Jersey, uses peer conferencing in all her classes in various configurations: one-on-one as well as groups of three or four. She also encourages the students to make appointments with her—as frequent as they want—as the due date for a paper approaches. But she says it is the peer conferencing that often catches tense shifts, jerky transitions to quotations—a whole raft of pedestrian but useful points for mechanical correctness. She hands out sheets describing what grammatical and formal structural devices are expected of an "above average" high school senior paper, and her college-bound students assiduously work on one another's papers to help them attain that standard. In an extreme example, one girl had written an entire paper using the wrong name of a book's main character, an error the peer editor caught.

It seems manifestly true that much more writing and involvement with writing take place in a classroom where students are editing one another than if the teacher is acting as copy editor for every draft of every paper that gets written, and it seems to me that copy-editing is *not* the best use of a teacher's time. English teachers of junior high and high school students have suffered long enough on Sunday nights with huge stacks of papers that they correct in great detail and great frustration, knowing full well that the students will flip through the paper for the grade at the end and never look again at the painstaking corrections—unless there is an opportunity to rewrite, a chance to raise the grade. It seems sensible to me to have as much copy-editing and checking as possible (for spelling, punctuation, sentence structure) done in class—by other students.

The active nature of peer editing makes for a livelier English class. Students can, of course, do much more than copy-edit one another's work. Students can learn to ask all the right questions: Could you tell me more here? Wouldn't it make better sense if . . . ? Adolescents, like all children, thrive on each other. Edna Patton speaks of a student who was what she called "creative but jumbled" until the girl became involved with a new boyfriend who happened to be an excellent writer. After they had been together a few weeks, the girl's essays, in and out of class, were suddenly smoother, better organized, and more articulate. What caused the change? Was it the salutary effects of love? Or was it the opportunity to observe a well-organized writer at close range? Was it just the right moment for everything her teachers had told her to come together? "Sometimes," Patton says, "someone just explains it a different way, and the student gets it." The teacher's job, then, is not to find any one way of helping students get deeper into their work. The teacher's job is to offer many ways—inspiring lectures, private conferences, small groups of students—maybe even an introduction of two kids who might strike up a friendship that will improve their writing.

Teacher Chris Schorr also emphasizes the relationships between the teacher and the student in one-on-one conferences:

> If the piece is bad, but it's the best the kid can do, my responses are softer and more encouraging. If it's crap because they gave it no time or thought, I tell them it's crap, and I won't give them credit. At some level, I have come to believe, crappy work is a test of the teacher. The kid wants to know if you can tell the difference between good and bad work—and if you can, how much do you care about the good stuff? Enough to make a fuss? (Not everyone likes me, though—surprise, surprise). But I think part of the confidence they have to have in you is confidence that you're telling them what you really think—and that you have confidence in their ability to do it well themselves—eventually. . . .
>
> I often tell kids that I can't write personal stuff, and I tell them how much I *LOATHED* "sharing" my stuff in the writing courses I've taken. I keep intensive stuff to *pairs* or to myself and the student mostly because I can't bear to read my own stuff out loud. I know of other teachers, though, who work well with groups, "sharing" and critiquing.

I like the fact that Chris Schorr recognizes the importance of the relationship between the writer and the person who is responding. The relationship between teacher and student is complex: the teacher is giving a grade; the student may or may not want to be writing; they may not get along very well. It is especially important for the more powerful party—the teacher—to be conscious of the relationship. Chris, of course, also points out the other side of it: the student can be testing, flattering, manipulating the teacher too.

In high school, the people who respond to your writing are not of your own choosing, generally speaking. In college, when you're required to take a composition course, you usually don't choose your teacher. Even when someone signs up for an elective such as "Beginning Your Novel," the course I teach at New York University, the students generally don't know me. I think, then, that it's important for teachers to be aware of their own preferences and prejudices in writing. I try to tell students my biases early on and suggest that in certain situations they take what I have to say with a sprinkling of salt.

I say all this about relationships between writers and their teachers (including peers who are helping them revise) because I think there is nothing more important in revising than learning how to give and how to get useful responses to your work. In the teacher-student relationship with younger children, the burden of making this exchange falls on the teacher. For people in college and up—anyone, really, who is writing of his or her own volition—the burden of making a good relationship for revision falls on the student as well.

The people you take your writing to are going to influence you, willy-nilly, so be careful to choose good readers. If you are writing on your own, and a friend or colleague offers to read your work, seize the opportunity, but think ahead. Consider the likely biases of your potential reader. Does the potential reader enjoy many kinds of books? Maybe he or she only reads mysteries and crime fiction, whereas you've written something slow and full of interior mood description. Try to come up with specific questions to direct the reader's response to your writing. Ask, "Does this remind you of any other writers you like? Are there parts where you lost interest? Which parts held your attention best?" Or you might say, "I know this is rough, so I don't really want to know if the language sounds bad, I just want to know if the hero sounds like a jerk. Would a woman like my heroine go out with a guy who acts this way?" After a leading question like that, you might get a discussion, an argument even, but you are also more likely to get at least something specific you can mull over and use.

This is a particular problem if your readers are reading more out of friendship to you than out of a general interest in literature. For such readers, you might ask, "Please tell me the things that stuck out most in your memory. Does it seem like real life to you?" Or better

still, ask them to comment on something they actually are knowledgeable about. Say, "Listen, could you pay particular attention to
the baseball game and tell me if it sounded like real baseball?" It is
dangerous to your ego to ask global questions such as "Is it good?" or
"Do you think I'm a real writer?" I often find it useful to say something like "Listen, I'm eager for some response to this, and I would
love to have you read it. But please read it rapidly—I'm not at the
stage where I want to start polishing it up word by word. I would particularly like to know what you as a man think of the main character:
does he seem like a fourteen-year-old boy to you? And how about the
mother? Is it believable that she would say what she says?" In other
words, know your reader, and know what information you need.

The more experienced you are as a writer, the easier it is to become your own responder; that is, by separating yourself from yourself through time, you can read almost like a sympathetic stranger.
But even when you become good at having some distance on your
own work, you will sometimes want a warm body, a receptive smile,
an open ear. A writers' group has been an important part of my writing life for the last ten years.

Groups can function in different ways: some are strictly critiquing sessions, others focus on support. Ingrid Hughes describes a supportive group in which each member has up to fifteen minutes of
uninterrupted talking about writing. "This time [for the writer] to
present her feelings without premature responses that may cut off
their full expression is safeguarded from interruption till [she] has
finished talking."[1] The group I am a part of is somewhere between
a support group and a critiquing group. We do use the go-round in
which each person talks with minimal interruption, but our focus is
on reading our works-in-progress. Our group has seven writers who
meet every two weeks except during the summer. We take turns
reading aloud and then discuss the pieces. Some groups provide
each other with copies of the work to read in advance or during the
meeting, but we have found that we like the particular insights that
come from hearing the words. Sometimes we also ask one another
individually to read more nearly finished manuscripts. We discuss
general problems of our lives as writers. We eat a hearty meal and
enjoy one another's company.

---

[1] Ingrid Hughes, "Writers' Group," *New Directions for Women,* Spring, 1979.

For me, the group is especially good at picking up places where there are problems in my writing—they don't always have solutions to the problems they detect, but if a majority of them hear something wrong, I know I have to take another look. Sometimes we have as much fun as a class of fourth graders writing a silly story about the clock eating the teacher, and sometimes we are as serious and stringent as the best deep revision and fine editing. For an aspiring professional or avocational writer, or for a teacher of writing, such a group can be invaluable. What counts is regularity, enough people to know there will always be a group, some agreed-upon ground rules, and—above all—an atmosphere that is honest but supportive. This is tricky, of course: it is important not to be merely kind, but, on the other hand, a peer group is not the place to hone your wit at the expense of another's work.

TRY THIS: If you write on your own, find a group. Organizations for teachers such as the various Writing Projects encourage this kind of networking.[2] Many writers take classes in continuing education at colleges in their area primarily to find like-minded writers. Organizations such as the National Writers' Union and Poets & Writers have publications with classified ads that include writers' groups.[3] Other people find like-minded writers at writers' conferences and writers' colonies.

As I was drafting the proposal for this book, I took an early draft of the introduction to my writers' group and asked them to listen to it not for infelicities of language—I was far from ready for editing— but to tell me what it made them think of, to share some of their thoughts about revising that might help me think deeper. In other words, I used my colleagues to deepen my preliminary thinking about my book. We had a discussion about revision, and I was impressed at the time by how much variety there is in the way writers approach their own writing—and the teaching of writing, because over half of the people in the group are also teachers. Eva Kollisch, for example, a professor at Sarah Lawrence College in Bronxville, New York, said that when a student's work isn't good, she asks the

---

[2] Each state (and some cities) has its own Writing Project.
[3] National Writers Union, 799 Broadway, New York, NY 10003. Poets & Writers, 72 Spring Street, New York, NY 10012, also has publications listing writers' workshops and conferences.

student to talk it, to tell her what he or she wants to say. The student's talk often has clearer ideas and better language than the written version. Eva notes down what the student says, then gives the notes to the student. "Here, this is what you said out loud. Something was going on and you didn't say it on paper." This is a time-honored and important way of encouraging another person to go deeper: talk it through. Then Eva laughed and said, "But I can't do it to myself, unfortunately!"

Several people in my writing group emphasized the importance of "hearing voices." That is, you need to hear your own voice—to be able to talk your way through a piece of writing aloud or in your mind—but also, for fiction writers and poets especially, to hear the voices of people from your memory and of your invented characters.

Sybil Claiborne, a member of my writers' group and the author of three books of fiction, says, "If I can hear the right voice, I know I'm on the right track." Once she ran into a problem, she said, when she had to make a nonfiction presentation in public. She didn't have a voice to use and didn't know how to find one. She became terribly angry at herself.

"Well," we asked, "how did you get out of the trouble?"

"I wrote it," said Sybil. "I wrote my way out."

She found a way of saying *what* she had to say by writing, and through the writing discovered *how* she wanted to sound for this particular presentation. For Sybil, finding the voice is the first foray into the deeper realms of what she is writing. It is for her, she says, the hard part, even the main part. She likes what comes after: "I *love* revision," she says. "The first draft is horrible—illiterate garbage. But at least it's there. Revision is a collage . . . in the finished product you can hardly see the original draft. It's a sort of building up and building up till something comes out of it."

Suzanne McConnell said, "I can say ditto to everything Sybil says except that I can't stand it—the first draft is so horrible, I hate to look at it. I have to learn to trust myself all over again as a writer, and finally I do."

"Yes," agreed Carol Emshwiller, "it's like I don't know how to write—I feel that all the time."

For experienced writers as well as for beginners, revision can be fun or it can be excruciating, but is always there, a part of writing, early, late, and always. Other people can offer companionship through the odyssey of revision as well as concrete suggestions on how to do it.

TRY THIS: If you are having trouble with a piece of writing, tell it aloud to a friend, and then try writing again. You can either ask the friend to take notes on what you said, or tape record it, or simply remember your own voice the next time you write.

TRY THIS: Think of some simple incident from your childhood, something good or something embarrassing, perhaps a time you were hurt. The only requirement is that it be brief. Tell it for a friend or a tape recorder as flatly and factually as if for a police blotter. Now tell it again, as if you were including it as an example in a chatty speech for colleagues: tell it as a story. Try it a third time, as if it were a fable or a story for children. See how many voices you can develop.

TRY THIS: Do the same exercise in writing.

TRY THIS: Have a friend read what you have written. Have him or her ask you questions about anything and everything. Is there some detail that seems to be missing? Something not clear? Answer all the questions, even if they seem to take you on a tangent or to make what you've written too wordy. It's better to start with too much material than too little.

One of the most important things the exercises in this book can do is offer ways to revise by gathering more material. The next chapter is about that quintessential phase of deep revision—adding more.

Chapter Five
Going Deeper by Adding

After the first burst of inspiration, you usually need to add more. The purpose of adding to a piece is not merely to make it longer, nor is it merely to flesh out an idea or (perish the thought!) pad it. The real reason to add is to get farther inside, to find new directions, to get a clearer understanding of your material. If all you ever do in writing is draft, correct your spelling and punctuation, and make a fair copy, you are at risk of merely hovering over the surface of your material. When I think of going deeper, I always think of mining: you tunnel in, dig out the ore, and eventually smelt it to separate out the metal.

Fortunately, going deeper by adding more material is probably the easiest thing for a teacher or editor to ask. It is intrinsically flattering to the writer to say, "Wait a minute, this is so interesting that I want you to tell me more about it!" For beginning writers, or writers who are inexperienced, revision by adding can be as simple as staying at the desk a little longer or coming back to the piece a second time. Sometimes the question "What else?" or "Was there more?" helps a writer realize that, yes, there *were* more details or incidents. Leroy Jackson, a student at Weequahic High School in Newark, New Jersey, wrote this brief paragraph on the first day of a workshop:

> This morning the basketball coach call Roy down to his offices and said, After school we have a game, do you want to play? Roy said yes I'll play. At 1:30 the baseball coach call Roy to the main office and said, We have a game at 3:00 at the park. Roy wanted to play in the basketball game, but he didn't want to let the baseball team down. So he had to make a decision after school.

When I asked him on the second day simply to continue—to *make it longer*—Leroy first did a little editing by adding quotation marks and putting past tense endings on his verbs. Then he added a second paragraph.

This morning the basketball coach called Roy down to his offices and said, "After school we have a game, do you want to play?" Roy said yes I'll play. At 1:30 the baseball coach called Roy to the main office and said, "We have a game at 3:00 at the park." Roy wanted to play in the basketball game, but he didn't want to let the baseball team down. So he had to make a decision after school.

Roy thought to himself that the baseball team had enough people for the game, and the basketball team wanted him to play, and he wanted to play. So when 2:30 came, he told the baseball coach that he wanted to play basketball, so the coach said that "Since we have twelve people you can go play basketball." At the basketball game they won, and he had twenty points and seven rebounds, but the baseball coach was mad at him.

Often inexperienced or young writers don't have a sense of how much the reader needs to know: the writer has a complete image in mind of a description or action or event or argument (Leroy knew about the baseball coach being mad at him, but I didn't), and they are surprised that their writing didn't convey the whole thing to the reader. I often say to a young student in a workshop, "What happened to your dog is exciting, but I was just thinking, I have no idea what kind of dog it is—I figured he was a little curly gray poodle." "No!" says the child. "No, it's a German Shepherd named Arnold, only we didn't know when we first got Arnold that he was a she!" "Well," I say, "you should write that in your paper. That's interesting—and funny too!" A major step in revision, whether it is done by a young child or a high school student or an adult making a presentation or writing a novel, is to make the work fuller, more expressive, *more interesting*.

Thus children don't mind going back over what they've written if someone really wants to know more about it and treats them as what they are—experts on their own real lives and imagined experiences.

TRY THIS: Pick up the piece you are working on, and add more, even if you thought you were done. Explain what came before, or talk about what might happen in the future, or simply add something you left out. If your brain says, "But I'm just repeating myself," or "But I already said this," don't worry. You are probably saying it a slightly different way, perhaps a better way—and even if not better, then at least you'll have two choices when you come to the final draft. And don't forget that if you do come up with something new, you can put it wherever it seems to fit best.

TRY THIS: Do the same exercise, but add more at the beginning—some background information, or historical context, or something that came before what you've written so far. This is especially useful for fiction or personal narrative and often gives you new insights, if not new material, but it can be useful in setting up nonfiction too.

TRY THIS: Lay aside whatever you have been working on, and go on a brainstorming mission by using Timed Writing. This has many names—Free Writing, Directed Free Writing, Automatic Writing, etc. The principle is simple. You lay aside your usual methods for writing, and set a timer for five to fifteen minutes. Write whatever comes into your head (free or automatic writing) or whatever comes into your head about the piece you are working on (directed free writing). You might want to write about what is bothering you about the piece or what you left out of it and why you left it out. You should follow any tangents your mind goes on. This is a real fishing expedition, aimed at stirring your brain and seeing what comes up. The only rules are that you don't go back to correct or change what you've written, and that you keep writing the entire time.

TRY THIS: Pick up something you started earlier in the year (or an old piece from your files) and read through it rapidly. Turn it over so you can't see it, and write a new ending or beginning or both using Timed Writing. Don't look back again at the first draft until you have written for a while. See if this way you can get back into it, deepen it, say things a new way.

Professional writers also need to add more information, and one of an editor's most important jobs is to say, "I think you didn't give enough information at this point." For example, once when a science fiction writer friend of mine read a draft of my science fiction novel, she asked, "But how did those human beings get on that planet in the first place? How long have they been there?" I could answer some of her questions, and others I had vaguely hoped to get by without thinking them through, but I found that answering her questions helped me a great deal in clarifying my ideas and coming up with new ones. Specific requests for more information by good readers help an author both to improve the piece in question and to learn how to make a fuller draft the next time.

Emily Klinker, one of my Expository Writing Tutorial students, a ninth grader from Gambrills, Maryland, drafted the following personal narrative:

> "Hi! My name is Emily. I'm a compulsive liar." Sounds crazy, doesn't it? Well, that and "stupid" probably fit my description best when I was about three or four years old. I was the faithful sidekick of my older sister Alice. We did everything wrong and then made up the stupidest lies on the face of this earth to cover up. Amazingly enough, this very habit of lying through my teeth was probably what taught me never to lie unless in a life-or-death situation.
>
> It wasn't that I was defenseless. Heavens no! If I was in a position to be spanked for some heinous crime or other, I would start laughing hysterically and running around the legs of the appointed punisher. It worked, too. At the sight of some little tiny kid laughing and running in circles with a ridiculous expression on her face, the avenger immediately let down her guard (it was usually Mom) and started laughing right along with me.
>
> Now, the problem was that Alice got into more trouble than I did. My idol, I decided, was not going to get hit more often than me even if she did deserve it. Ever since I had the capability to talk, I covered for her. If something bad happened and Alice was the suspect in question, I wasted no time. My immediate response was always, "I did it." Don't even ask me what possessed me to do something that stupid to save someone who would go ahead and do the same thing again anyway. To this day even I don't know.
>
> I used the same ploy every time. It worked for a while, too; I got hit, Alice got off scot-free. It was great. Then my parents caught on. I took the blame every time, and they knew I was more well-behaved than my sister. It just didn't fit. So, they turned the tables on me. I admitted to the dirty deed every time, but every time, Alice got hit anyway. I just didn't get it. She even got hit for stuff I really *did* do! Parents ruin everything!
>
> Well, I figured it wasn't any use lying for Alice if she was always punished anyway, so I started telling the truth. It worked! They believed me because I blamed her more often instead of always blaming myself, and she only got in trouble for things that were really her fault. I was so happy because she only got in trouble for what she really did that I ignored the dirty looks I got as she was spanked and told the truth regularly. The weird thing is that to this very day, the habit still sticks— well, most of the time, anyway.

This is an example of a good student writing quite well. With energy and humor she recounts a family story that—as she told me in a letter—is often repeated around the family dinner table. In fact, it seemed to me to be a case of a family knowing the story so well that they need only the briefest reference to remember the whole situation in all its amusing detail. I found myself wondering, though, exactly what sorts of "heinous" crimes those four-year-old sisters actually committed. My critique was simple: "Give me some examples. Tell me more."

Here is Emily's second draft, with the enriching explanatory material in italics:

> "Hi! My name is Emily. I'm a compulsive liar." Sounds crazy, doesn't it? Well, that and "stupid" probably fit my description best when I was about three or four years old. I was the faithful sidekick of my *near-twin sister, Alice.* We did everything wrong and then made up the stupidest lies on the face of this earth to cover up. Amazingly enough, this very habit of lying through my teeth was probably what taught me never to lie unless in a life-or-death situation.
>
> It wasn't that I was defenseless. Heavens no! If I was in a position to be spanked for some heinous crime or other, I would start laughing hysterically and running around the legs of the appointed punisher. It worked, too. At the sight of some little tiny kid laughing and running in circles with a ridiculous expression on her face, the avenger immediately let down her guard (it was usually Mom) and started laughing right along with me.
>
> Now, the problem was that Alice got into more trouble than I did. My idol, I decided, was not going to get hit more often than me even if she did deserve it. Ever since I had the capability to talk, I covered for her. If something had happened and Alice was the suspect in question, I wasted no time. My immediate response was always, "I did it." *For instance, my sister and I always collected lightning bugs in the summer. Well, one year we were allowed to keep them overnight, AS LONG AS THEY STAYED IN THE JAR. Well, after bedtime, we decided it would be just great if we could divide the bugs up between the two of us and keep them with us under the covers for night-lights. It didn't work out at all. When our parents came in later to check on us, they found a room full of free, blinking-in-the-dark, lightning bugs flying all over and two little monsters trying desperately to fake sleep. You guessed it! "I did it." My parents were trying so hard not to laugh over the catastrophe which had just occurred that I almost didn't get a smarting reminder on my backside. I was too tired to activate my "dancing" defense. At least I got Alice's sympathy vote.* Don't even ask me what possessed me to do something that stupid to save some-

one who would go ahead and do the same thing again anyway. To this day even I don't know.

I used the same ploy every time. It worked for a while, too; I got hit, Alice got off scot-free. It was great. Then my parents caught on. I took the blame every time, and they knew I was more well-behaved than my sister. It just didn't fit. So, they turned the tables on me. I admitted to the dirty deed every time, but every time, Alice got hit anyway. I just didn't get it. She even got hit for stuff I really *did* do! *For instance, I will cite a case which was not resolved for a long time due to lack of evidence. We had a van, which we got around the time when my dad went into business for himself. Running his own business meant he had lots of pads full of yellow paper, some of which he kept in the van. The van had many vents. I, the five-year-old Daddy's girl, decided to help Daddy; I took all the little scraps of paper stuck to the spines of the yellow pads of paper in the van off the pads and stuffed them, one by one, into the heat ducts. Nobody saw me do it. Then the heater stopped working. Mom and Dad got it fixed, and I didn't see the connection. No problem. Then the heater broke down again. I cost my parents a total of five hundred dollars by "helping" them?* Of course they blamed Alice. I didn't get any credit. It wasn't fair. Parents ruin everything!

Well, I figured it wasn't any use lying for Alice if she was always punished anyway, so I started telling the truth. It worked! They believed me because I blamed her more often instead of always blaming myself, and she only got in trouble for things that were really her fault. I was so happy because she only got in trouble for what she really did that I ignored the dirty looks I got as she was spanked, and I told the truth regularly. The weird thing is that to this very day, the habit still sticks—well, most of the time, anyway.

The point of the essay is the same, and indeed the essay is almost identical to its first draft except for the addition of two incidents and the information about how close Alice and Emily are in age. The elaborations are not, however, decoration without function. It is the precise quality of the high jinks that gives the reader a flavor of what this family is really like.

TRY THIS: Take an essay or short story you wrote at least a month ago and read through it. Then close your eyes and point your finger *arbitrarily* into the middle of it, and, at the end of the sentence or the paragraph nearest your finger, write "For example," and add a narrative or other example that backs up what you are saying.

Sometimes with a group of teenage, college, or adult students, I read aloud a passage that seems to me to need more information and then ask everyone (including the author, either anonymously or not) to respond in turn with more details—how they imagined the character looked, what kind of car it was, etc. Everyone can come up with a different specific for each general word. The point is made that if you want people to see what you saw in your imagination, you have to add information. Sometimes, if the writer really hasn't imagined this particular bit very fully, new ideas from the other people will help fill in the blanks.

Some sophisticate with a text on literary theory in the back pocket of his black jeans might say, "But that's exactly what I wanted, for the reader to make up his or her own mind. The reader is more important than the author anyway. I want it to be the reader's decision." Whether I agree with the theoretical assertion or not, *my* point is that for those who *do* want the reader to know what made their families laugh instead of simply that they did laugh, then it is necessary to include examples.

Often I take my drafts to my writer's group and ask for exactly this kind of response: "What do you think will happen next, or what do you think this character's motives are?" In this way I can simultaneously test my work—does the group think the character is motivated by greed rather than love?—or find out if *I* am the one mistaken—that it really *is* greed that is motivating the character. And maybe I should add greed to my character's motivations. Thus I end up learning more about the very character I've created.

TRY THIS: Read aloud to a friend a passage that is too thin (seems not to have enough information or simply seems to need something and you don't know what). Have the friend ask questions.

TRY THIS: Do the same exercise, but ask the friend to take the piece home, read it at leisure, and then *write* the questions. This may allow for a more formal and searching set of questions.

TRY THIS: To help deepen a character in a novel or short story, try adding any of these for the character: a memory, a dream, or a flashback to an embarrassing incident.[1]

---

[1] For more ideas on enriching and adding to fiction, see chapter seven, "Deep Revision and Fiction."

TRY THIS: Read a piece of nonfiction again, looking for a reference you need to look up. Add a piece of information from the encyclopedia or other source (a bit of historical background, a date, the name of a city).

TRY THIS: In your piece, find a word whose meaning has always been a bit elusive to you. Use a good dictionary, and see if the meaning of the word gives you any ideas for further additions that would deepen the meaning of the idea where the word appears.

TRY THIS: Go through a piece—nonfiction profits from this as much as a poem or story—and add colors, sounds, or metaphors in at least three places.

TRY THIS: Go through your piece looking for every time the following words appear describing a thing: *nice, big, good, bad, old, young.* Now replace each of them with a complete sentence that is as specific as possible in describing that thing.

Are there ever times when you add too much, go too far? Do you ever have too many examples, too much detail of the sort I've been encouraging you to add? My answer is not a simple yes or no—rather, I would maintain that, yes, you certainly can go too far, add too much, but no, it is almost never a mistake. First of all, you can always cut later, and it is generally more fun to work with a manuscript that has too much material than one that is skimpy and needs to be filled out.

Going too far is usually fruitful, because it can give you new projects and new thinking even if it is too much for the piece you are presently writing. Some of my stories, essays, and even books have grown out of material excised from an early draft of some other work. We always have many ideas, and when we go off on a tangent, the tangent has a good chance of being important for another project, even if not for the one at hand.

When I was fourteen I wrote "The Mutants," a story set after the Third World War. I was gripped by that story: I doodled pictures of the characters in the margins of my school papers, fantasizing about the events in it. I had a wonderful time writing it, then went back and tried to act as I thought a writer should act, by polishing. When I reread it now, I am impressed with its callow but vigorous integrity. You would never mistake it for the work of an adult, but you don't get bored. Although the story was really finished, about two years later I decided to add more.

I was older, knew more, had experienced more, read more, but I was still drawn to the material. My original draft had a beginning, middle, end, and some pencilled-in polishing. When I came back to it at sixteen, I was still caught up by the drama, the theme of intolerance, and the heroic girl, but I had also become sophisticated enough to think I knew what was meant by a Great Novel, and ambitious enough to think I could write one.

I planned a new draft that would be large and serious. It would have more scope, more points of view, more characters, would cover a greater time span. The original story, all in first person, begins like this:

My name is Vili Yarrow. I am a mutant. . . .

and the whole story continues in that first person, autobiographical voice. My new, more ambitious draft was to have three introductions as well as its real first chapter:

(Introduction Number One)

The Time Machine

Suppose that you have invented a time machine. Suppose that you have visited the past to your heart's content and have seen with your own eyes the great men doing great things. Suppose that now you decide to go forward in time: not far, only a handful of decades. . . .

(Introduction Number Two)

A Brief History of the Sovereign City-State of Glacier

I, Thomas Jefferson Scott, librarian of the Glacier City Library, am writing this history for future generations. I realize that I shall never complete this history due to my advanced age, but it is my earnest hope that my son, Robert Browning Scott, will continue after my death. . . .

(Introduction Number Three)

The Ugly People
An excerpt from the epic poem by the same name composed by Whisty the poet

We are the dregs
The muck beneath their feet.
The beasts
The subhumans

Not fit to suck the teat
Of our mother,
The Earth.
For she is not theirs alone.
To us, also, she gave birth.
She is our mother too!
I, a creature, say this,
And it is true.

Chapter One

Hunt Yarrow strode up the street of Glacier to what had once been the Royal Moving Picture Theatre and was now the Glacier City Government Building. The early spring morning was bathed in equal parts of brilliant morning sunshine and mud. Two little boys were happily flinging mud pies at each other. They paused when they saw Hunt and cried in unison, "Hi, Mayor Yarrow!"

It is a sort of sampler that shows off what I knew of narrative styles. But with so many pages of introductory material, I ran out of energy long before I reached the actual adventure. My long beginning and experiments with voice and point of view wore me out. After a few efforts to restart the project, I lost interest and stuffed it in a manila envelope.

When I compare the two projects now, I find the story I wrote at fourteen to be a much better version: limited, but authentically imagined. The unfinished, more ambitious second version is much farther from achieving its goal than the less sophisticated first version. I wasn't ready to write a full-scale novel then. Still, when you expand your reach, grasp for something farther than you've gone before, while you often get a handful of air, the very expansion of the muscles makes it easier to reach and grasp the next time.

This is part of deep revision too: the reach that goes too far, the additions that don't belong. It pays to file everything. Even the second version of the story that I called "The Ugly People" has turned out to be useful—in this book!

Another situation in which it is important to develop strategies for adding more material is when you are well into a long project and begin to lose steam. Assuming that you really want to continue, or perhaps *have* to continue for an assignment, the problem of adding more can also be a problem of finding strategies for priming the pump and getting yourself rolling again. Perhaps you have been away from the work for a while and now have to get back into it. This is especially a problem for writers working on long projects—usually adults, but some advanced students as well.

Anyone who writes a long project—a thesis, a major research paper, a long story, or a novel—can't depend on bursts of inspiration. You won't have enough, and they won't last long enough. We all need ways to keep ourselves and our projects going. How, above all, to restart yourself?

One mundane way to add more to a long project is simply to create a daily routine that brings you back into your writing. The daily act of writing itself, such as in a journal, can prime the pump. Another way to get restarted for adding more is to do a little polishing of yesterday's work. Cut out a phrase that seems awkward, add an adjective that seems better, tinker around until suddenly (and here comes the part that is maybe unconscious, maybe developed with experience) there will be a new idea—maybe just a small one—but a small qualitative leap to another level. The very manipulating of words seems to activate the brain, to move us from one mode—doing business teaching a class, or taking a class—into the writing mode.

TRY THIS: Take whatever you wrote most recently and for a limited time—five minutes to a half hour—polish it, adding words, cutting words, changing words. Putting a time limit on it is important. Then, at the end of the time period, make yourself stop polishing and begin to add.

TRY THIS: Try a timed or automatic writing to get your pen scratching. Use the timed directed writing that I described above, writing *about* the project you are trying to restart, get back into, or make longer.

For younger writers, a teacher who writes with the class (models the act of writing) is a big help. Visits from writers are a lot of help, too, especially if they can talk about when writing is difficult for them, and how they get themselves going on revision. There are any number of filmstrips and videos of authors who talk about their writing process. In a Public Broadcasting System television program some years ago, Eudora Welty was shown in her dining room spreading out the typed pages of a story. Using a large pair of scissors that she identified as her sewing scissors, she cut the pages up and rearranged the dialogue, took a snippet of description and put it over here, physically moving her sentences and paragraphs from one place to another.

TRY THIS: Look at a couple of films or videos of writers at work, or talk to a writer or poet. The writer can be a local reporter for the newspaper or an aspiring, unpublished poet, or even a high school or college student who could talk about how to get back into writing a paper for a class. What is needed is to hear how various writers go back into their work and add to it. After you have a few samples of how writers work, try one of their techniques and see if it works for you.

TRY THIS: Do another timed writing. Start this one by closing your eyes and visualizing a reader of your work. Is it your husband? Wife? A friend who shared the experiences you have decided to write about? Picture the person in detail. Then set the timer and write that person a letter in which you discuss how you feel about the project you are trying to get deeper into. Does it feel like a weight on your shoulders? Is there some part you are looking forward to getting at? Some incident or point you've been looking forward to describing or making but haven't gotten to yet?

TRY THIS: Try reimagining something concrete from your writing—an image, a particular moment in time, an example you referred to but didn't dramatize. If the senses can be aroused, the emotions will usually follow—or rather, they will already be there, inextricably woven together with the senses.

TRY THIS: Sometimes what is needed to get back and get deeper into yesterday's writing is simply to focus. Try closing your eyes and imagining a blank screen, if you're working on a story or drama. See before you the events from yesterday, and then continue them into today.

TRY THIS: If you are working on a poem, clear your mind by breathing deeply ten times, and then relax and listen for the poem.

Chapter Six

Changing Media for Deep Revision

Sometimes what you're writing needs radical reworking—more than just adding on or getting feedback from a reader. Sometimes a piece needs to be overturned, plowed under, perhaps left fallow for a while, and then approached in some new way. If you are in a real hurry, one quick fix is to switch from revising by eye to revising by reading aloud.

TRY THIS: Read your piece aloud. Listen to the sound of your sentences. If they feel like tongue twisters in your mouth, the words probably need smoothing out on the page as well. If the sentences seem too long, they probably need shortening.

Reading aloud gives you other angles, a sense of the rhythm of your sentences, and a way of catching rough spots. When you get a new angle on a piece, you may find that whether you read it aloud or lay it aside for a week, what is supposed to be a book review is turning into an essay. Or perhaps you started out writing a poem, but the images turned into long sentences, and it occurred to you that you were really writing autobiography. These things happen all the time. If your writing or your students' writing seems to want to be something other than what it started out to be, give serious consideration to trying it in another genre or medium.

Often research can deepen one's understanding of a piece of writing or move you forward with new ideas. Thus, if you are writing an article or story set in 1955, and you get stuck, you might go to the library and skim old *Life* magazines. Any new information can have a beneficial effect on your writing: you'll be able to visualize your scenes better if you know what kinds of cars people drove in the year your story is set.

I know a writer who flew to California when she needed to go deeper in revising her novel. You could call this research, I suppose, though in her case, I think research on places and layouts of towns was much less important than sense impressions. She wanted to smell the air and see the color of the vegetation on the hills near Monterey, to let a physical engagement with the place give a jolt to her writing. As a result, new scenes did come to her, material that explained why characters had acted as they had. In a smaller way, I stimulate my thinking when I move my hands to experience the very gestures I am describing.

TRY THIS: Using your body, feel out a scene or image you are working on. This can mean something as simple as going in the kitchen and eating a peach like the one in your article, or it can mean taking a walk and being again in the place you are describing or one like it, or it can mean physically acting out something you are writing about.

TRY THIS: If you are having trouble with a scene in fiction or personal narrative, try drawing it.

TRY THIS: Do it as a storyboard—that is, the visual representation on paper of a script for film or television. Or try it as a comic strip.

TRY THIS: Another quick fix exercise for going deeper is to leave the work and go to a museum or art exhibition. It's fine to take a break and go for a walk or to the movies, too, but the point of this exercise is not to take a break, but to change the level of your writing. If your wheels are spinning in your project, an experience of art may give you the traction you need. Walk through painting galleries, try to give yourself to the visual experience, and then go back as soon as possible to your writing and see what comes out.

TRY THIS: Listening to music can also work, but avoid music with words.

If you teach young children, a number of the following exercises offer some easy ways into revision. With younger students, there is no way to overemphasize the importance of mind-body unity—the more parts of brain and body you can get involved, the more intense the writing will be.

TRY THIS: Have a class write *from memory* about a local park or zoo or pizza parlor or even the school auditorium. Then take a walking tour and observe the place directly, taking notes and writing on the spot, if possible. A day later, back in class, write again, making additions and changes based on the observations.

TRY THIS: Have everyone look at the three different descriptions of the place, choose the best parts, and combine them into one piece.

TRY THIS: Another version of the above exercise is to do it as a group writing. This can be a poem or a prose portrait.

TRY THIS: A variation on this is to draw the on-site observation instead of writing it, or record the sound of it. Then return to the classroom and write.

Moving back and forth among the literary genres can also do interesting things to a piece of writing. A book editor once told me about receiving a beautifully written manuscript that just didn't hold together as a novel. The editor took the manuscript and broke it up into linked short stories.

For several years a woman who had been in my novel writing class had been trying to write a novel based on certain formative experiences of her life, and she wrote extremely well, but was dissatisfied with her dialogue. Her characters didn't say much to each other, and when they did, they tended to sound stiff. In order to work directly on this problem, she prescribed her own cure and signed up for a playwriting class. In it, she told me, she was forced not only to write dialogue, but to act out her own and other students' plays. The emphasis on dialogue and building a dramatic scene also improved her novel enormously: what had been a beautiful but sometimes vague writing style was suddenly sharpened by the sound of real voices and dramatically advancing action. I would be willing to bet that the physical involvement of acting out her own writing and others was part of the change in her writing, too. She seemed to have learned to feel from the inside the rhythm of a scene—how long it is, how it builds, how it reaches a climax and plays itself out.

A watershed in Henry James's development as a novelist came after nearly ten years of rather unsuccessful playwriting. At the end of that period, his novels had taken on a whole new aspect and were organized on a principle of the dramatic scene. I now suggest the following option to many aspiring novelists: if dialogue and drama don't come to you naturally, try a playwriting class. Change media. Easier still, if you are having trouble with the logistics of a scene, have some friends act it out for you. Observe how long it takes them to walk across a room, to open a door.

Carol Emshwiller, who teaches short story writing, uses an actor's exercise for character building. She has students picture a doctor's waiting room where a character looks at a magazine, gets a drink of water, sits back down. How would each individual in your story perform these mundane activities? A new discipline can open up practical techniques. The very act of pulling up stakes and trying new territory can add fresh ideas and strategies, new depths.

For younger kids, group dramatization can be a wonderful means of expanding and exploring writing. Once when I was presenting the idea of conflict to a class of sixth graders new to fiction writing, I had them act out a couple of simple skits to suggest things to put into fiction: tones of voice, facial expressions, gestures. The idea was to improvise a skit based on the situation of an older person on line in a fast food restaurant who gets bumped by a teenager. One intense student, John, took charge of his improvisation. He chose to be the older character, and immediately transformed himself into a frail old man, complete with mimed cane and mouth sucked in over imagined toothless gums. Another boy, Chris, played a sort of generic teenager with a bopping walk and a sneer. He bumped the old man hard, and John shook his cane and muttered something funny about young people today. They did a nice job and gave me ample material for discussing how, if you wanted to put this story into narrative prose, you would have to describe the cane, the man's stoop, the teenager's attitude, etc. During the discussion, Chris started revising his performance: "I should have made the boy more like a punk," he said from his seat. "I should have made him say 'Yo!' and stuff like that."

My writing assignment was for the students to close their eyes, visualize a conflict, and write it, including gestures, voice tones, etc.

They could either describe a new scene or use the one that had been acted out. When we got around to reading aloud, John raised both his hands, begging to act out his piece, which turned out to be a revised, expanded version of the skit. In his new version, the old man was the same, the teenager a little more of a punk, and a third character entered with his hands in the now-ubiquitous police-gun position: "Nobody move! This is a robbery! Everybody get on the floor!" The punk fell flat, and the old man lowered himself slowly, always in palsied character. Then the robber aimed his gun at a girl and demanded her money. As she was handing it over, the punk grabbed the robber's legs from his prone position, and Old John half rose and began to beat the bad guy with the cane! The old guy and the punk had joined forces to subdue the villain. The robbery was thwarted, and the old man waved his cane: "These young people today!"

John had clearly expanded and completed the skit that had given him so much pleasure: his kinetic involvement and his obvious passion for acting powered the writing. The next step is for John (or his group) to write in all the added material—the extra characters, a description of the robber, the woman who hands over her purse. The final assignment is for the students to take the play and revise it into a story, giving background information and projecting into the future.

TRY THIS: Hand out one-sentence skit starters to small groups: siblings argue over who does the dishes; a teenager bumps an elder in a public place; a sibling finds that a younger sibling has borrowed something without asking; a young person comes in after curfew and is caught by a parent—anything with a conflict that students can identify with. First, act out the conflict using improvisation, then have the small group go back and write the pieces, as acted, or with new ideas, in dramatic form.

TRY THIS: Do the same exercise, but instead of writing the plays in groups, do them individually.

TRY THIS: Instead of using skit-starters, use pieces the class has written for another assignment: stories, poems, or narratives from real life. Arrange the students in small groups and have them take turns acting out the pieces as written. Then have everyone go back and make new versions of their pieces, after they've performed them.

Suggest they add gestures, ad-libbed lines, or anything else from the performance.

TRY THIS: Do this same exercise using non-dramatic, non-fiction pieces, such as opinion essays. The students will have to come up with a way of dramatizing or illustrating their ideas. Afterward, perhaps they can add the scenes as examples or illustrations of their points.

TRY THIS: Assign watching t.v. and writing a script of the show that was watched. This is a good opportunity to discuss cutting, close-up and establishing shots, etc. The exercise teaches the students how television is structured and helps them take control of t.v. a little through understanding how it works.[1]

I use conflict as a starting point in a lot of these exercises because conflict is at the heart of almost all fiction, as well as drama. There are plenty of poems with dramatized conflicts, particularly dialogue poems (such as May Sarton's "Cut and Knife" and Robert Frost's "Home Burial").

TRY THIS: Write a description of a real-life conflict. This could be either something you observed or something you participated in. It could be humorous, serious, in-between, or all three. Draft the conflict rapidly, then revise it in the form of a play. Have it acted out by the class or some friends, then add anything that your actors did in gesture or expression. Also add any ideas that come up in discussion before or after the skit.

Then either continue it as a play—changing reality and adding things that didn't happen but might have—or continue it in fictional form, expanding and lengthening so that different possibilities unfold.

A group of high school students at Chestnut Street School in Newark, New Jersey, did this exercise. The Chestnut Street School specializes in helping female students stay in school after they become

---

[1] Standard formats for the various types of scripts can be obtained in various places, but Writer's Digest Books has one called *The Writer's Digest Guide to Manuscript Formats* that covers all the bases. For more information, write them at 1507 Dana Avenue, Cincinnati, OH 45207.

pregnant and just after they have their babies. One girl I'll call Francine wrote the following passage:

> The conflict I once had was between my mother, boyfriend, and I. My mother didn't approve of me seeing him, less on me birthing his child. So they went on and on, which made me go on and on. Finally it was stopped when I moved in with my boyfriend, although I know it's still in the hearts.

Francine was obviously writing about a major event that had dominated her life for much of the recent months. The paragraph refers to the conflict, but says very little about how she felt. She wrote the piece in what she probably considered school prose, and she ran out of steam pretty quickly. At our next session, I asked the class to use their conflict paragraphs as a treatment or story idea for a dramatic piece. I had the students close their eyes and imagine their narrations as if they were happening on television, then write them as scripts.

Setting

My house in Newark, NJ—a bright yellow & green house and quite cold day.

Characters

My boyfriend (JAMAL)—*tall, dark, and handsome.*
Me (FRANCINE)—*medium height, light-skinned with brown hair & eyes.*
My mother (LINDA)—*fat, short, but very attractive.*
My son (BOO-BEE)—*newborn, light-skinned & very handsome.*

ANNOUNCER: It began on February 29, 1991, around noontime. Francine, Jamal, and the baby was sitting in the sitting room watching television and admiring our new three-day-old baby. So Francine's mother Linda came home and walked straight to the sitting room where Jamal, Boo-bee, and Francine was.

LINDA: Hello, everyone.

JAMAL: Hi.

FRANCINE: Hey, Mommy.

LINDA: So Jamal, when do you plan to return to your job?

JAMAL: Well, I'm going to see if I still have one tomorrow being's that I took off so many days for Francine's labor.

LINDA: Well, that's what you get. You should have went to work because bringing in the money to take care of everything is more important than some labor.

JAMAL: Well, you may feel that way because none of your men came in with you, but I feel that seeing my first and only child born is very important and special.

LINDA: Well, I tell you this much. If you don't get your stuff together I'm going to have something real special for your birthday.

JAMAL: Meaning what?

LINDA: Try child support, not seeing your child, or not calling or coming over here.

JAMAL: YOU DON'T HAVE THE RIGHT TO TELL ME WHAT I CAN OR CAN'T DO WITH MY CHILD!!

LINDA: Oh yes I can.

FRANCINE: (*yells*) Please you two stop it.

LINDA: And you get out of my house you **%!!** etc.

JAMAL: ***%!!** you, you ***%!!** etc.

ANNOUNCER: So Francine watch Jamal run out furious and she cried and cried. When she tried to call him, her mother ran her off the phone. So finally that night, Francine's mother went to work, and Francine get in touch with Jamal. They planned to leave the next day. So Linda came home trying to be friendly and Francine still was mad. So, when Linda left Francine packed and moved in with Jamal. Which Linda was PISSED OFF! But, she learned to accept and forgive so now everyone is OK.

You'll notice that after the big scene, Francine goes back to straight narration, using the announcer as a narrator. At this point she is ready to draft in script form scenes two and three and so on, should she decide to continue this as a drama.

Equally well, she could do a second draft that would turn the whole thing into a piece of fiction or a personal narrative. The possibilities with a piece like this are many: the students hugely enjoyed acting it out in front of the class, and it could even be produced as a class project. Or the story could now go back to fiction, using descriptions of the tones of voice and the gestures that the girls used when they acted it out. It could become a group effort, since it seemed to speak to the girls' experiences pretty directly. It could also become an essay that begins with the concrete narrative and dialogue of what happened and then discusses in a more generalized way the situation of teenage parents.

TRY THIS: As an extended project, make a collection of your students' conflict pieces, giving different versions of each piece in several media, including scripts for drama and scripts for radio plays and teleplays as well as fictional narrative.

TRY THIS: Make a video of one or several of the pieces and see if this gives you ideas for changing the written form.

TRY THIS: Try one as a comic book. This can be an illustrated version of the story you are already working on. Or try it from the other direction: study some comics for typical formats—the shape of the boxes, frequency of dialogue, etc. Make blank format pages for students to fill in with their stories and drawings, and then try turning one of these into a story or play.

TRY THIS: Try a *fotonovela*, the comic-book format story with photographs instead of drawings. Photograph dramatic moments of the story, then type the dialogue and cut it out as balloons pointing to the speakers. Stories of passion and revenge are most typical.[2]

TRY THIS: Have a Media Day and show how many ways the same narrative can be presented. You might include a comic book by one group, a music video by another group, a novel by a third, a live play by a fourth.[3]

---

[2] See my article "Spinoffs: Fotonovela and the Marriage of Narrative and Art" in *Teachers & Writers*, vol. 8, no. 1, a special comic book issue.

[3] For a theoretical discussion of how narrative works in various media, see Seymour Chatman's *Story and Discourse* (Ithaca, N.Y.: Cornell Univ. Press, 1978).

*   *   *   *   *

Some Notes on Computers and Revision

I'm going to end this chapter with a few ideas on how computers influence—and can be used in—revision. Just as drawing the scene instead of writing it, or changing from the written word to the spoken word, or acting out a narrative rather than writing it has observable effects on the kinds of ideas that come out, so do the actual physical tools and materials we use. Visual artists are particularly aware of this: they find the same subject coming out very differently in charcoal or gouache or oil paints.

Similarly, although perhaps more subtly, the different tools we use for writing have different effects. I have mentioned the way reading a piece aloud can give new insights into how to revise it. There are poets who like to write on paper napkins in bars, and novelists who can't find inspiration without the long yellow legal pad. John Milton dictated his great religious epics to his daughters, and Thomas Hobbes is reputed to have written on his bedsheets. Like many people, I began writing stories by hand, then switched to a typewriter. Now, although I do almost all my work on a computer, I like to make at least one go-through with a pencil on the manuscript, because the change to wood and graphite in my hand gives a different rhythm and flow to my writing.

At the same time, it is also important to me to be able to see the work more or less as it will look to a reader. With a novel or short story I like to flip through the manuscript to see if it seems dense in narrative or if there is a lot of dialogue. I would not necessarily add dialogue just because the manuscript looked too dense, but I would consider it.

It has been more than ten years now since newspapers began using computers in the newsroom for easier editing. Freelance writers began to purchase them for home use as soon as the price became reasonable. The freedom of never having to type a clean copy again is for most writers well worth the price of the machine. I began writing this book, for example, by typing in certain samples of work and quotations that I knew I wanted to use. They were stored in the computer as examples I didn't have to change. No matter how many times I revise my own words, I am spared the tedium of retyping those paragraphs of other people's words. When my fingers hit the keyboard now, I am adding ideas, moving sections to a more logical position, making changes to go deeper, not simply performing the mechanical task of retyping. Everything mechanical is easier with a computer: for instance, as I'm writing, I keep a special file for my bibliography, and as I come up with a new book for it, I insert it in proper alphabetical order. The computer's word processing program even takes care of my footnotes, automatically changing the numbers if I move them. I confess there were times in the past when I weighed a revision based on whether I had time and energy to retype a page on the typewriter. Revising has always been part of the life of my writing; retyping was always a little death. Computers have made revising immeasurably easier.

TRY THIS: For a first try at composing on a new computer, write some extensive journal entries. Then try a few friendly letters, and a business letter. Work into composing creative work on the computer gradually—only after you're sure you know how to save new material.

Using a computer has its negative aspects, too, which have interesting ramifications for revision. The major one I've found is that word processors tend to be so easy to use, and the touch of the keyboard so light, that I often use too many words. I have to edit out more unnecessary prepositional phrases and adverbs in my writing now than I did when I was writing more slowly and did more editing in my mind. Many writers find that, on a word processor, it's hard to stop polishing again, it is so easy to insert some new words, erase some old ones, that they say they never get to new writing because they are having so much fun tinkering with the old.

But overall, using computers does improve our writing skills. My husband avoided writing not because he had no ideas but because he was inhibited by fear of making errors. He had never taken a typing course, and in his efforts not to make a mistake in a letter or report, he would use catchphrases or even clichés rather than his own voice. But when he began to use the computer, first as a hobby, he came across a program that used video game techniques to teach the proper fingering for the keyboard: the enemy fires j's and f's at you, and if you find them fast enough with your proper fingers, your city isn't destroyed! Once he learned to type more rapidly, he began writing longer, friendlier letters. Freed of the fear of making errors, his personality could come through in his writing. With the possibility of easy corrections before having to commit himself to a "hard copy" (printed-on-paper version), he suddenly became looser, more conversational on paper. He could experiment and be playful.

My husband's experience is quite typical. A pharmacist I know who is well into his sixties bought a word processor recently. He immediately began writing short stories, something he had always wanted to do, but had never tried until he had the machine. Something about the machine itself seemed to invite him to try something new. Young people now come to us in high school and college who have been composing on computers for years. Very early on, they are able to develop a facility with restructuring their papers through the cut-and-paste function of word processing. (The essay by Expository Writing Tutorial student Emily Klinker in chapter five was done on a computer, which is one reason she could add material so painlessly.) I find it interesting how some students' work appears to leap higher in maturity when it comes through a computer. This is partly because the printed composition is easier to read.

Witness, for example, what happened in the two follow versions of a paper by another EWT student, Josh Davis. The assignment was to write a process analysis paper telling how to do something. He wrote the first version by hand (because his computer was in the shop), the other directly on the computer.

First, my assignment:

December 14

Dear Joshua,

I'm glad your finger is back in action, and I look forward to the computer too—I have a feeling you write longer pieces when you have your keyboard. . . . Which brings me to Assignment #7, which is due January 18, and will be the second essay in the narrative form. In general, I am attempting in this course to assign you some of the most important "rhetorical forms" of nonfiction: description, narration, and argumentation. Most first-year college composition textbooks follow this plan. Today's assignment is a sort of sub-form of narration, the PROCESS ANALYSIS essay. I want you to write an essay describing someone in the process of doing something. This could be a profession, a craft, an activity like dancing or skating, or anything else, serious or humorous. The main point is to observe the thing being done very closely, tell in detail how it is done, and, if possible, try to get a sense of the person doing it too.

Meanwhile, enjoy your holidays!

Sincerely,
Sue

Here is his response:

On the Purchase of a New Game for MY COMPUTER

1. Select a game that suits your interests, pick one quickly, because after this we're going home. (To play continuously.)
2. Rip the bag containing the game out of your mother's (or father's) hands.
3. Race through traffic (even though your parents are close behind) and be waiting at the car long before your parents arrive.
4. Once in the car take the game out of the bag and toss it to your mother, who will open it.
5. On her returning it, rip the plastic off and dump the contents on your seat.
6. Find the instruction booklet and read (skip to next step if the trip is short).
7. Tell your parents how wonderful they are and how great the game is.
8. On arrival at your house, exit the car and run into the house, if your mother hasn't gotten there earlier to unlock it, jump through the window if you must.
9. Rush to your computer and do what you must to start it.
10. Note: Do not accept any food or offers from parents that might take you away from the game.
11. At this point, the game won't work. If someone is around, tell them that you know what is wrong. Slowly open the instruction manual and read. Try again.
12. You now have a few choices, you may: cry, scream or, which is the most profitable, get angry at your parents for letting you buy the game.

I wrote back:

January 11

Dear Josh,

Your How-to Essay was really pretty funny. I was afraid there would be a problem with the computer game when you described all that excitement (including climbing through the window. How about in instruction #9 saying what you *do* to start the computer—turn the switch, call up whatever at the A prompt or however your machine works. Also, #10 could be expanded a little—make up a typical offer that might come from your parents: name the sandwich or drink or other suggestion they make. And isn't there an instruction missing between #11 and #12 (which is very funny)? Shouldn't there be an instruction where your frustration builds up—maybe tell what the game program does that shows it isn't working: does it give some particular screen repeatedly? Anyhow, expand that part just a little to build up the frustration before the final scream and cry instruction.

I'm making fairly elaborate suggestions for this because Assignment #8, due February 1, is to be a revision.

Sincerely,
Sue

Here is Josh's revised version, this one typed on his computer and printed out for me. Notice how much fuller and funnier it is:

1. Select a game that best suits your interests, and make sure it is worth the money that you will shell out. (If it is a present, it really does not matter.) Choose one quickly, but stay focused on choosing one that you will like. Furthermore, the sooner you choose, the sooner it will be paid for, the sooner you can open it—and the sooner you can play it.

2. On exiting the store, demand the bag containing your game from whichever parent is holding it. On receiving it, rush ahead.

3. Race through the streets, barreling over pedestrians and dodging traffic. (Ignore the screams of your parents.) Be waiting at the car door for a long time before your parents come. (A comment about their slowness pisses them off and makes them want to get away fast—which will get you home even sooner.)

4. Once in the car remove the game from the bag and attempt to open it. Unable to open it, toss the bag to your mother. (Or your father, even though he may be driving—if he has sharp fingernails.)

5. Once your mother (or father) returns it to you, remove the excess plastic, open the box, and dump the contents on the seat next to you.

6. If it is a long trip, find the instruction manual and skim through it. (If you are lucky enough not to have a long trip, skip this step—starting the game without any knowledge of it is more fun.)

7. Be most gracious and kind to your parents, comment on how much you love them and your newly acquired game.

8. Exit the car before it even comes to a stop, run to your house. Do anything possible to get inside. (Jumping through the window IS permissible.)

9. Rush to your computer, slam the disk into the drive. Change the current directory to the corresponding drive and Start the game.

10. Do not accept bribes from your parents which may keep you away from your game. Common mistakes are made by the creative and deceptive parents, who think up many preposterous ideas along the lines of not having anything to eat for hours, or that you have to go to bed for school. NOTE: For the most important reason, including sickness and blood, one may leave the computer, but any more than five minutes will ruin the total enjoyment of the game.

11. Upon reading the message announcing the failure of your game to start, sit back and wait a minute. If a person is in the room with you, assure them that everything is alright. Try again, and on receiving the same message, make sure everyone in the room (including you) is sure that it is the company's fault. Never, ever let on that it might be your fault—and beyond a doubt it can NOT be the computer's. (This might make someone come to look at it, take it away, and you will be computerless for a month or more.)

12. Once everyone else has left the room, try again and again to make it work, use everything possible to make it run. (Short of hitting the computer.) Turn off the computer and sit on the floor.

13. At this point a few options will come into mind, we suggest you do not do one that might result in damage to a person or your computer. The best choices seem to be to cry, or to scream as loud as you can. However, the most profitable choice is to blame your parents for this situation because they let you buy the horrible game.

TRY THIS: Take some piece you are interested in getting into again, and write versions of it using any two or three of these methods: by hand (not copying over, but from memory); by typewriter; on the computer; by dictating to a friend or family member; and by speaking into a tape recorder. When you are finished, transcribe the versions into identical typed or printed formats and see what differences you observe.

TRY THIS: Choose the best sections, sentences, and paragraphs from the above and combine them in one final draft.

TRY THIS: If you are using a computer, or learning to use a computer, do the previous exercise using the cut-and-paste function of the computer.

TRY THIS: Spend a little time on the computer rearranging paragraphs. What would happen, for example, if you moved your conclusion to the beginning? Some summaries actually make better beginnings than conclusions because they map out the essay in a way that clarifies things in advance for the reader.

The computer can loosen up a tight writer; it greatly eases the mechanical tasks of retyping and preparing footnotes; and it is a wonderful way to experiment with rearranging your work. In particular, computers lead to a kind of experimentation that is much harder to do without the speed of electronics. I am thinking of a quick trial like the last exercise above, in which you give some rather radical restructuring a whirl. In the last chapter of this book, there will be a discussion of large-scale restructuring that depends heavily on the use of a computer. I'll end this present chapter with a few more computer revision exercises that are especially useful in revising fiction.

TRY THIS: Try using the global-replace function in your word processing program to change every occurrence of a proper name. What happens if New York becomes Metropolis? Or, if your character's name is presently George, see how it would be if he became a Reginald. What other changes seem to be required by such a substitution?

TRY THIS: Go all the way through a manuscript using the global-replace function to change Reginald (a male hamster) to Fatima (a female one). Now go back and revise with this new gender. What does it do to the plot? Are some events totally changed by gender?

TRY THIS: There will be more in future chapters on experimenting with point of view, but global-replace is a way to give a quick try to a few pages in first person instead of third, or vice versa. Do you like the story told in the new way?

Chapter Seven

Deep Revision and Fiction

Techniques for getting a new angle are important in all types of writing, but they are at the heart of writing fiction. At some level, fiction writing is nothing but new angles: a revision of real life that asks "What if?" What if it had turned out differently—if a man under certain circumstances had been faced with a certain dilemma and acted in one way rather than another? Fiction writers use "What if" to penetrate layers of experience and observation and meaning, to see what is underneath. When this process is working well, the writer is probably not even aware of it, but simply sees something unfolding: a story, the meaning of the story.

When I ask children to tell me the difference between fiction and nonfiction, someone always volunteers confidently that nonfiction is true and fiction isn't. Then I make a great show of disagreeing: "What? Haven't you ever read a story or a novel that seemed to be as true as nonfiction? Didn't you ever learn something from a story?" The students usually respond by naming particular books and authors that have moved them, having known all along that there is a truth beyond that of fact. In my own writing, even when I make up a story, I am always trying to get at something true. That is not to say I write only serious things, for even frivolity provides insights into the way things are. The word *fiction* itself, while sometimes used to mean lies or falsehoods, comes from the Latin verb meaning to shape, fashion, or mould—to put in order something that already exists. I like to think of the "made" quality of fiction rather than its "made-up" quality.

Much of what we accept and assume as fact has also been re-made and reinterpreted. History is continually being revised to suit current ways of thinking, and even the most ancient religious texts are interpreted by each new generation. Making is something human beings naturally do, and fiction is part of this activity: an imaginative reinterpretation of experience.

"What if" thus becomes an essential tool as well as a game. In writing fiction, poetry, and plays that use experiences from my own life, I always wonder "what if" I had made the other choice. Or, as Peter D. Zivkovic ends a poem:

Went to war, then college.
Learned stuff.
Loved every moment.
Got married, then.
Became a teacher.
Had kids. Paid
taxes and premiums.

Kids grew up and left.
Oldest died young,
thirty. Cancer.
Other two got married.
One was arrested first.

I retired, a widower.
Two swell grandkids.
Never did win the lottery.
Finally died.

All because
one day in the rain
I'd found Robert Frost.
Him and his
two damn roads.[1]

Science fiction is an obvious case of taking some facts and examining them by pushing them to extremes in an imagined future or alternative world, but the past can be reimagined too. Even mysteries, thrillers, romance novels, and other genres offer a world view that revises real life by giving experience a form, a comforting sense of closure and solution, when life itself is so often open-ended and unresolved.

---

[1] Peter D. Zivkovic, "Autobiography: Or How I Grew Up Never Vacationing at Bar Harbor in the Summer or Palm Beach in the Winter," *Dog Days,* 1992, English Dept., Fairmont State College, Fairmont, WV 26554. For the entire poem, see appendix.

The next writing exercise is for adults or children, and it contains its own built-in deep revision. It begins with a chunk of real life that it revises and What Ifs into a short story.

TRY THIS: First, DRAFT. Write down as rapidly as possible a scrap of dialogue you have overheard or participated in. It can be recent or from the past. It may be as ordinary as a conversation about new curtains for the teachers' lunchroom, as silly as a couple of kids on the playground making jokes, or it can be serious—a parent-child conflict, or an intriguing bit of gossip overheard in a restaurant. The point is not to worry about the content of the dialogue, but to transcribe rapidly the words said. Keep it unedited, just as it was said.

Second, ENRICH. Go back to what you have written and add details to the beginning, middle, and end. Write in the margins, between the lines, cut the paper in two and paste in a blank sheet, or use the cut-and-paste function on your computer. The objective is to add material *throughout* the draft, material such as sense impressions. (What gesture did she use as she said that? Was it hot that day or cold? What sounds were in the background? What did his cologne smell like?) Describe a setting, people, actions, tones of voice, thoughts. Include narration to give background. You can stick to your remembered observations, but you can also embellish or speculate. This process is both a means of adding and expanding, and a way of going deeper—slowing down time, as it were—and re-seeing or re-imagining.

It is important to break this into two steps, first the rapid capturing of dialogue (drafting), then the more leisurely recapturing (enriching).

The third step is to FICTIONALIZE. Continue the scene by playing What If. Make something happen that didn't happen in real life. If it was a dialogue in which you were involved in a conflict, allow yourself the fun in your fictional extension of saying what you would have liked to say and didn't think of. Give it a happy ending, or a funny one, or simply an ending that is more interesting than what really happened. Don't forget that fiction does not require the landing of the Martian Marines: even speculating as to someone's thoughts is to fictionalize.

Obviously the above is not the way every fiction writer writes. It is meant to be an exercise, a concentration of the processes of fiction.

To me, among the most important types of What Iffing are those that fall under the general category of point of view. That is, even when a person is writing memoir or autobiography, the voice that speaks is not the same as that of the actual writer. No matter how honestly the writer describes memories, he or she is still revising, changing, editing. For instance, if I were to reconstruct what happened to me when I was a child, it would not be simple or even straightforward. One of the things fiction (and often poetry) can do so well is to accentuate this very difference between the actual writer and the persona on paper to create distinctions and possibilities.

Fiction, in particular, often involves imagining the actions of people unlike oneself or pretending to be someone else. Another of my favorite revision exercises is one I call the Outside-Inside, in which you describe a person physically, from the outside, and then an interior monologue or "inside." (I referred to this exercise in chapter one and then described a version of it using drawing for first graders in chapter two. In the form I'll describe here, the Outside-Inside works as an extended assignment for upper elementary school students and older.) Like many of my exercises, it begins with description: even when creating a character, or imagining a character's interior life, it's usually good to begin with physical details. You may end up cutting much of this kind of detail, but it serves an important purpose by making the subject more alive in your mind.

TRY THIS: WRITE A DESCRIPTION of a real person in objective or at least exterior terms, emphasizing details. Describe how the person looks, sounds, even the texture (feel) of his or her hair and skin, the smell, etc. Be as detailed as possible. This works best if it is someone you don't know well but have observed, perhaps someone who lives on your block, or one of your teachers, or someone you play sports with occasionally.

Next, skip a line or turn over the page, and WRITE THE PERSON'S THOUGHTS. Use first person ("I wonder, I think, why does this always happen to me?") to imagine what it would really be like to be inside your character's head.

Come back on a different day and read over what you've written. What could happen next to this person?

Here are a few examples of student pieces:

Teo Linda

She has white hair, soft, wearing black dress. Is not strong, fashion designer. Friendly, cheerful, old, funny, sweet, wears glasses. Artistic, pale face, brown eyes, great big smile, accent.

My thoughts are: I love to draw, I'm very lonely because all my brothers and sisters and parents and cousins are all deceased. I'm in a Home. I feel like I'm punished for something. I don't know what for.

—*Amy Fromkin, fifth grade*

*　　*　　*　　*　　*

Her nose is overly prominent and her jaw is undershot which gives her the appearance of a mouse. One can about picture the whiskers twitching on each side of her face. Her hair is a mousy brown to go with her face and is bopped. The curls are arranged so that when she turns her back, one might imagine another face watching one's every move. Her choice of clothing is a turtleneck under vee-neck sweater with a full long skirt that turns to follow her every time she moves. As she raises her hand, one might expect her to wave daintily at a friend in the back row, and so it seems until a full-chorded sound fills the room. Quickly she cuts the sound off with a motion reminiscent of wiping a stubborn stain off the kitchen counter.

Monologue:

I'm standing on the stage of the auditorium. In front of me are about 150 talented singers, on my right is a pianist, and behind me is the audience. I can sense their anticipation as I raise my hands in the air to begin. I feel every eye on me and take a deep breath, not only to calm myself, but almost to breathe in the excitement of the night. Very gracefully I turn to the pianist to give her a tempo. My hand ever so gently waves "1-2-3, 1-2-3" and I nod for her to begin. Next I turn to my lovely choir and raise my hand ever so slightly to bring them in. As I raise my hands, so their voices grow louder. My control is absolute.

—*Carrie Schurman, eleventh grade*

TRY THIS: Do the same exercise, but rather than use a real person you have encountered, describe a person who has been in the news lately. Make up the details you don't know (color of hair, type of shoes, how tall), and proceed as above. Do the same thing for a rock star, a political figure, or a historical figure.

TRY THIS: Of course, you can also do this by making up a character from scratch.

TRY THIS: A further extension, which is a good lead into revising this fragment into a short story, is to put the character into action. Have him or her do something, and describe the action and then write the thoughts of the character in action.

TRY THIS: Add a dialogue in which the character is involved in a conflict with someone else.

TRY THIS: Try this same sequence of techniques on a story you have already drafted: describe a character in greater detail, write a monologue, and then write a character's thoughts as he or she is in action. Add a conflict in the form of a dialogue.

By this point, you will have viewed your character in several different ways and will probably be far from your original "real life" material. In their book called, appropriately enough, *What If?: Writing Exercises for Fiction Writers,* college-level creative writing teachers Anne Bernays and Pamela Painter offer several writing exercises that focus on fleshing out characters in a story.[2] One is simply to take a sheet of paper and make a lengthy list of facts about the character: name, nickname, vocation, sexual history, character flaws, pets, food preferences, etc. Bernays and Painter are quite emphatic that you should do this only *after* you have written your draft. They also suggest deepening and reconceiving a character (after it is written) through creating a milieu for the character—home, social class, etc. Every teacher of creative writing has a store of these exercise suggestions, and many of them are especially apt for going deeper not only into a character, but also into the structure of the work itself. Here are a couple that I use in my novel writing classes.

TRY THIS: Make a detailed questionnaire for your most important characters in order to find out about them. Do you know their ethnic groups? Do they believe in a supreme being? If so, do

---

[2] Anne Bernays and Pamela Painter, *What If?: Writing Exercises for Fiction Writers* (New York: Harper Perennial, 1990).

they pray? To make such a list, see the Bernays-Painter book, or get together with friends who write and together create your own questionnaire of things you think would be useful to know.

TRY THIS: Use the list mostly as a means of getting to know more about your characters, but try adding at least two of the new details somewhere in your story. Don't simply say, "Oh, by the way, Jared was raised a Presbyterian but converted to Judaism when he married his first wife." Rather, see if you can slip in this information in a way that doesn't disrupt the flow of the story.

TRY THIS: Describe a room or place as it looks to one of the characters in your piece. Now describe it again as it appears to a second character. They will notice different things, and have different reactions to the same things. This can be done either in first person or third.

> It was rush hour, again, Monday morning, on the 7 train from Main Street. I decided to take Richard with me. This was 3 days after he arrived from South America. The car was packed wall-to-wall. There was no air on this 85 degree morning. Obviously some passengers hadn't taken a shower. The usual garbage was on the floor, with one difference—someone had spilled coffee all over the floor. Great. Loud music was coming from a teenager's Walkman. Did they predict rain? They must have, 'cause several people were carrying umbrellas. Except me.
>
> Richard seemed hypnotized by the activity. He was watching the pretty Latin girl sitting in front of him. She was sustaining his gaze. Above her, a Spanish ad caught his eye. "Fascinating!" he thought. "Thousands of miles away from home & I can still read an ad about foot pain in my own language. How can one car hold so many people? Where is everybody going? And who's got the Walkman?" he wondered, as he tried to place the singer's name. Was that Colombian coffee he smelled? Smells can bring back such pleasant memories. . . .
>
> —*Diane Medina, NYU School of Continuing Education*

I want to reemphasize that these analyses and deepening methods should *follow* drafting. That is, get as much of your story out as you can first and then use these techniques for deepening, expanding, and figuring out where to go next.

It must be clear by now that I agree with those writers who say that writing *is* revision. At almost every stage except the very first bursts of inspiration and drafting, there are layers of revision that take the writer in new directions that become new paragraphs, new chapters, sometimes even new books. The more I write, the more I find my revising intertwined with my composing.

One of a fiction writer's essential problems is to find the best way of telling the story. After I have drafted a story or a couple of hundred pages of a novel, I often come back to reread and rethink whether or not I am telling the story from the point of view that goes deepest into the material. At this point, some of my considerations and techniques begin to resemble what critics and English professors do. I ask myself some questions. Who is the narrator telling this story? How close is the narrator to me? Does she have the same autobiography as I do? Did she vote for the same candidate for president as I did? The way we and our characters witness life is not, of course, an academic question. Our world views are different not only because of our physical positions in space and time, but also because our whole life histories predispose us to experience in radically different ways. Fiction writers make much of this knowledge of the discrepancy between the various possible points of view.

The more similar the main characters in your story are to you the writer, the more difficult it is to clarify these distinctions. For example, when I am writing in the first person, it is essential for me to understand the distance between me, Meredith Sue Willis, and the "I" in my fiction. Frequently I establish very carefully in my mind where the "I" and I differ: instead of assuming that the narrator is like me, I will make small but important changes so that she has a different hair style, is an only child instead of a sibling—all small details that help me see the world from a slightly different angle, and thus imaginatively see what I might not have seen had I stayed too close to myself.

In one of my novels, I went through several changes in establishing the point of view. The novel was the third in a series, the first two having been told in the first person by a character very much like me. In drafting this third novel, I found myself tired of the informal and somewhat self-absorbed young woman's voice, and I decided to follow my own advice, by switching point of view. I wrote a second draft of the novel in the third person, and I had an increasing sense of the main character not only as an individual struggling for autonomy and self-understanding, but as an individual in a context: a person of a certain age, from a certain background, with certain limitations. This was of enormous help to me. It opened up the piece: what had seemed tight and fixed was suddenly fresh and loose, and I felt free to put in new ideas, new scenes. Then, having revised the book into the third person, I laid it aside for a while, and when I came back decided that I wanted it in the first person after all. This first-person version, however, was much different from the earliest draft, or from the first two novels: the same young woman is still the narrator, but she seems to be less self-involved, more aware of the world around her. I think my explorations in point of view hugely improved this book: it seems to have gained a world view that encompasses much more than it used to.

This kind of decision-making can obviously be a great struggle, and sometimes comes clear only after many drafts. We are sometimes cowed by the belief that authors have a magisterial, immediate, and total control of their material. This idea hampers new writers, especially adults, and makes them feel that the process of writing is one of being in control. At some level it is true that you choose each word you write, but it is a trivial truth that can lead to rigidity and the danger of falling too quickly into someone else's patterns—conventional plots, stereotyped characters, catch-phrases, and the dread clichés.

In fact, even the most accomplished and talented writers do not sit back comfortably in their dressing gowns and select a point of view or a tone as if fingering a rack of ties. They struggle and experiment, rarely getting it right on the first try. Often in this muddling and experimenting stage of revision, though, you will find the right way to tell the story, and once you have the voice and point of view of the story, you are usually much closer to discovering the shape and structure of the work.

With luck—sometimes in the first flush of drafting, but often not until after many false starts and many pages of drafting—a character in a story will suddenly seem to start to talk of his or her own volition. Writers often speak of the discovery of this voice in almost mystical terms—certainly as if it were out of their control. If a character in one of my stories suddenly starts to talk to me, I have trained myself *at the very least* to listen for a while and explore that character's voice or point of view. I may use these ideas on another project, or

I may discover that this character will change the direction of my project, or I may simply learn a little background on the character that will make that character's behavior more logical later on in my story. But part of the discipline of imaginative writing is to explore, even when—or perhaps especially when—the exploration threatens the neat plan you have made for yourself. The negative side, of course, is that these diversions and new ideas and tangents can take years to follow through.

Following the diversions, particularly the ones that suggest changing angles or points of view, can lead both to deeper understanding of the material and to new material and is thus a cornerstone of deep revision. It can also be fun—like trying on hats from a costume box. When I am in the early stages of revising my fiction, I often try different versions of the same story—or at least the opening pages—in first person, third person, and other forms.[3]

TRY THIS: Take a poem, short story draft, or fragment that you have written and make a new draft of it (or part of it) in a different person. If it is presently told "he said she said," then change it to "I." You might even try out a sentence or two that addresses a "you" or pretends that a whole town or generation ("we") is doing the talking.

TRY THIS: Try a few sentences in a different verb tense or mood: try present tense ("Napoleon stands on the battlefield with one hand stuck in his jacket. He knows the flea is there somewhere.") or the imperative mood ("Stand on the ladder and survey the garden. Climb down the ladder, being careful of the next-to-bottom rung").

---

[3] There are many forms of narration. In the first person, an "I" tells the story, and all that is known is what that one person could realistically know. Third person limited is basically like first person, except that it is told in "he said, he did." What is dramatized is only what he participates in or guesses at. His thoughts are told, but no one else's, unless he is speculating about them. Theoretically, there can also be second person (see Jay McInerney's *Bright Lights, Big City*), but this is most often just a quirky first person. Another rarely used possibility is first person plural, "We first became aware of the aliens in our midst during the town's Fourth of July celebration" (an example is Gabriel Garcia Marquez's *Autumn of the Patriarch*). Omniscient third person is all-seeing, like God: the story is told so that everything can be known. The voice telling the story knows how people look, what they do, and what they think, their futures and their pasts. Objective third person is where the narrator knows everything everyone *does*, but not necessarily everything they think. These are only approximate definitions: there are also other possibilities. Some authors also vary their point of view from chapter to chapter or section to section of a book.

TRY THIS: Take a draft or fragment and rewrite all or a small bit of it. This time, instead of changing grammatical tense or person, change the actual individual telling the story. Many classroom teachers enjoy the retold fairy tale exercise in which the student tells *The Three Little Pigs* from the point of view of the wolf, etc.

Isn't He HOT!

One Saturday, Sandy and Chanel were walking uptown to just hang-out. They were on the corner . . . Chanel looked up by the mailbox and said, "Ooooh . . . don't that boy look good!" "Which boy?" said Sandy, questioningly. "The one with the Raiders shirt. Girlfriend, he is CRUSTY!" she said with a street talk attitude. "But the one next to him isn't so good," said Sandy eyeing him down. "Let's go up there and see if they say anything to us." "Alright, then let's go." Sandy and Chanel were about to approach them when Chanel said, "Girl, you were right, that boy does not look good one bit!" "Yeah, I know, but neither does that other boy. Ewwhh! . . ." "Come on then, let's leave and go to the park then," she said, wanting to leave quickly. They walked by the boys and said, "Ugghhth . . ." and then left in a hurry.

Do They Think We Are HOT!

Last Saturday my friend and I went to town in Cranford. We were standing by Sweet Dreams Cafe and then I saw these two girls. I said to my friend, "Y-Y-Yo, aren't those girls looking at us?" in a questioningly voice. He said, "I'm not sure, but they're not bad, in fact they're pretty fine. . . . " "Alright, alright, be quiet, they're coming up here!" I said in a hurry to hush up. We checked them out and then saw them eyeing us up and down.

"Hell . . . o," I said, taking an interest. "Man, see what you did, they saw your face and turned away," my friend said with an interesting sneer. "Well, they said hello didn't they," I said with a snotty attitude. My friend told me to shut up. And then we ended not talking to the girls at all.

—Dawn DeLaFuente, sixth grade

The next example was written by sixth grader Jeff Bergin at the Livingston Avenue School in Cranford, New Jersey. Jeff had already drafted a dialogue with a conflict, and I asked him and others to rewrite the scene from another participant's point of view. Jeff went from the first person "I" to a fictional third person Chris, "to protect the innocent," he said.

This Happened at C.C.D. on a Monday by the Church

One day a kid named Chris called Bob Brillohead. Bob got very angry.

He said to Chris, "Shut up you *%*! You're such a jerk."

Then someone yelled, "Rumble." So Chris just joked around and said "Any time, any place." Then Bob punched Chris in the stomach and then in the ear twice. Chris punched Bob in the stomach and then Bob punched Chris's glasses off.

Chris charged at Bob and yelled, "You knocked my glasses off you *%*! I'm gonna kick your butt."

Chris then picked up Bob and threw him into the car and then punched him.

Then some lady comes out of her car and gets in MY business. Then she says, "Take a deep breath and count to ten."

Chris still thinks Bob is stuck on three.

I suggested that he revise a third time and try it from the grownup's viewpoint.

The Fight

One day at CCD on a Monday I saw two kids fighting against each other. It looked like a violent fight, so I decided to take action.

I got out of the car and said to the two boys, "Hey, I'm a teacher and I will not allow you to fight. Take a deep breath and count to ten."

My job was over, so I got in my car and drove to where the sun was creeping beyond the clouds.

I like the way Jeff imagines the adult's point of view, and especially how his adult pictures herself a sort of western hero, heading off into the sunset. It's silly and endearing at once—or perhaps it's Jeff trying to please the teacher with a little extra description.

TRY THIS: In any piece with two people, write an interior monologue for the person who is most different from you.

My Talkative Daughter

It was a rainy, Saturday afternoon. Crystal was in her room as usual tying up our phone line. What in God's name could that child always talk about up there for so long. I'm going to have to go up there and yell but I hate it so much. I wish she would learn to get off without me yelling.

I stomped up the stairs.

"GET OFF THE PHONE NOW! You've been on it for over an

hour!" She doesn't seem to be listening to me, that little brat. Oh no! . . . my other daughter Elizabeth! I promised I'd take her to the mall.

"Crystal, you just got lucky, but if you're not off the phone when I get back, you're grounded!"

—*Carly Kaplan, sixth grade*

TRY THIS: Try an interior monologue for both people in the scene or story.

TRY THIS: Suzanne McConnell uses the following exercise with her beginning fiction students at Hunter College in New York City. She asks everyone to describe a scene in which something painful happened to them. After they've written that, she asks them to revise their pieces to include the points of view of all the characters who appear in the scene. This forces the students to imagine what it was like to be the father, or the teacher, or whoever on that fateful day.

TRY THIS: Write an interior monologue for an object in the scene—a variation on the time-honored "My Life As a Pencil" assignment.

Writers can gain great insight into their work through point of view exercises. I remember one day of near-blizzard conditions when New York University almost shut down, and only a handful of students showed up for my novel course. Since there were so few students, we did in-class writing, and I had the luxury of sitting down and writing along with everyone else. The exercise was to write a monologue for a character in your novel who was causing you problems in some way.

In one of my novels, I felt I didn't know the main character's boyfriend (and this was seconded by my writers' group), so I decided to try him. I began with his thoughts about the main character and her personality, but then the idea came to me to have him remember a dream from his childhood. Ultimately I used this dream in the novel by having him recount it to the main character, and I finally felt I was beginning to understand the boyfriend.

TRY THIS: Write a dream or memory for some character you are having trouble with in your story. Can you work this into the story?

TRY THIS: Add a passage of dialogue to your story in which two characters tell each other about their pasts.

TRY THIS: Take some story you've drafted, and try it from the omniscient viewpoint, if you've used limited third person, or vice versa.

TRY THIS: Read a little of your versions to someone else and see which way seems to work better.

TRY THIS: If you're working on a first-person narrative, try a new opening paragraph using a different age for the narrator: pretend it is a young person telling the story very close to the time of the events. Now tell it as if the narrator were very old and recalling people and events after many years.

TRY THIS: Look at a third-person story. Can you establish how old the narrator is? Maybe you switched back and forth. Are the sentences short? ("She was a girl with brown hair. It always got in her eyes.") If so, the narrator is probably a child (or Ernest Hemingway). Try the opposite of what you have so far, or, if you go back and forth, see if you want to establish one style, one distance from the events and people in the story.

Thus in our creative work, we have the opportunity to challenge some of the pre-existing patterns in our minds. We can imagine what it would be like to be the Other—an elderly person if we are young; a female if we are male; an outlaw if we are law-abiding. In this way, deep revision becomes not merely a way to improve our writing, but a way to revise and deepen our thinking.

Chapter Eight

Revising Nonfiction with Techniques from Fiction

Many of the techniques and exercises I described in the chapter on fiction are useful in revising nonfiction as well. Speculating and editorializing have of course always been a part of nonfiction, and conversely many early works of fiction such as Daniel Defoe's *Journal of a Plague Year* masqueraded as nonfiction. A biographer might enliven a book by reconstructing dialogues and imagining the thoughts and motivations of actual people. The personal essay dates back at least to Montaigne in the sixteenth century, and among its noted practitioners were English writers such as Addison and Steele in the eighteenth century and Charles Lamb in the nineteenth. More recently, starting in the late 1960s, the so-called New Journalism has employed such devices as interior monologue, dramatized dialogue, and other elements of fiction to convey real-life events. The writer becomes the protagonist in the effort to get the reader to experience something firsthand. Norman Mailer has done a lot of this kind of writing (my favorite is his *Executioner's Song*). Crime especially seems to lend itself to this sort of work (e.g., Truman Capote's *In Cold Blood*). Joan Didion, like Capote and Mailer a skilled fiction writer, has written of political and historical situations in *Miami* and *Salvador*. Here is an example of this genre from Tom Wolfe's *The Right Stuff*:

> In the training film the flight deck was a grand piece of gray geometry, perilous, to be sure, but an amazing abstract shape as one looks down upon it on the screen. And yet once the newcomer's two feet were on it . . . *Geometry*—my God, man, this is a . . . skillet! It *heaved*, it moved up and down, it rolled to port (this great beast *rolled*!) and it rolled to starboard, as the ship moved into the wind and, therefore, into the waves, and the wind kept sweeping across, sixty feet up in the air out in the open sea, and there were no railings whatsoever. This was a *skillet*!—a frying pan!—a short-order grill!—not gray but black, smeared

with skid marks from one end to the other glistening with pools of hydraulic fluid and the occasional jet-fuel slick, all of it still hot, sticky, greasy, runny, virulent from God knows what traumas—still ablaze!— consumed in detonations, explosions, flames, combustion, roars, shrieks, whines, blasts, horrible shudders, fracturing impacts, as little men in screaming red and yellow and purple and green shirts with black Mickey Mouse helmets over their ears skittered about on the surface as if for their very lives (you've said it now!), hooking fighter planes onto the catapult shuttles so that they can explode their afterburners and be slung off the deck in a red-mad fury with a *kaboom*! that pounds through the entire deck—a procedure that seems absolutely controlled, orderly, sublime, however, compared to what he is about to watch as aircraft return to the ship for what is known in the engineering stoicisms of the military as "recovery and arrest."[1]

Wolfe hooks the reader by using the present tense and direct address, and uses sense impressions, lists of evocative words, and even comic book sound effects! Readers tend to react strongly to this writing—some love the energy, others are put off by the density and pyrotechnics, but most agree that it is not staid.

In the following piece of personal narrative by Heather Sanders, one of my Expository Writing Tutorial by Mail students, the assignment was to narrate an incident from real life when you learned something. Heather, an eighth grader from Barrington, New Hampshire, did not like the assignment very well, as you'll see in her letter:

December 31

Dear Ms. Willis,

I think that this assignment, number six, has been one of the my least favorites so far. I had trouble writing it, as you can probably tell after you've read it. I think there are two main reasons why I had so much trouble. One is that I always have trouble writing anything that has to do with me or has happened to me. The second reason is that I waited to write it over Christmas vacation, which I shouldn't have done because I don't especially like doing anything during vacation. Overall though, I had fun over vacation. I hope you enjoyed your vacation as well. I am not really looking forward to going back to school although we do have a roller skating party Wednesday and a dance on Friday, so it shouldn't be too bad. It will just be hard to get used to getting up at 5:30 again. . . .

---

[1] Tom Wolfe, *The Right Stuff* (New York: Bantam, 1984).

Notice that she has so much trouble writing about things that happened to her personally that she changed the names of the people in her piece.

A Time I Learned Something

"Really? I can't believe she actually said that!" Andi chatted happily with her best friend, Sarah, on the bus that afternoon. They had been friends for as long as they could remember, yet they had extremely different appearances and personalities. Andi was a short brunette, who was usually quiet and shy, while Sarah was tall, blond, outgoing and would often say things that Andi would never dream of saying.

It was a Friday, and although she had a history report due Monday, Andi wasn't the least bit worried about not being able to get it done. After all, she had her notes together, so writing a final copy should take her no more than two hours.

Soon, it was time for her to get off the bus, and, after yelling good-bye to Sarah, Andi started up the long driveway. After letting herself into the house, she grabbed a snack of a brownie and milk and then went into the living room to watch a little bit of MTV. When she had finished eating, Andi decided to get started on her report. She was eager to get it done so that she would be free to do what she wanted for the rest of the weekend.

Andi got up off the couch and walked into the kitchen where she had left her navy blue backpack. She looked inside to find her green five-subject history notebook, where she thought her notes were. After she had flipped through the entire notebook several times and still not found them, Andi decided to look in her textbook. They just have to be here somewhere, she told herself. It wasn't until after she had looked through both her textbook and notebook that she began to get worried. By the time Andi had searched through everything in her book bag, including all of her notebooks, textbooks, and folders, she was in a panic. Her mind raced as she frantically tried to think of where else her notes could be.

Suddenly, Andi jumped up off the hard tile kitchen floor where she had been sitting and stomped into the living room. She flung herself onto the couch, mad at herself for being stupid enough to lose her notes. Even if they were at school, Andi knew that by the time her mother got home it would be locked and everyone would have left for the weekend. She was not looking forward to telling her mother that she had forgotten her notes. Andi knew that her mother would not be pleased with her.

Yet when her mother came home she was more sympathetic than Andi had envisioned. Andi explained everything to her mother. She had been prepared with pages of notes and references, but she had been careless in leaving her notes at school. After Andi had finished explaining, her mother offered to type the report as Andi told her the information in the way she wanted it written.

As she told her mother the facts she had collected Andi was surprised at how much she remembered. Finishing her report took longer than Andi had first expected but, considering that she had written it from memory, it hadn't taken very long at all.

One of the reasons I particularly like this piece is that it is itself about a revision technique—Andi has to reconstruct her notes from memory. I would love to see the two versions of the same history report, one written from her notes and one dictated from memory. A teacher who is getting bored with the typical student compositions might try doing what Andi/Heather did.

TRY THIS: After students have a near-final draft of a composition, ask them to lay it aside and work with partners. Ask them to dictate what they remember to their partners, trying to keep it lively, then switch and take dictation. They shouldn't look back at their original drafts till the dictating is over. They can always correct research facts; the objective here is to *enliven* the actual writing—to make the style more conversational and less like passages from encyclopedias. Then ask them to compare the two versions and see if they can be integrated.

I made only a few small comments about Heather's paper, such as when she uses the proper name "Andi" where "she" would be less intrusive, and suggesting that certain details may be unnecessary— the color of her backpack and five-subject history notebook. What I really wanted to see was a stronger ending. She simply "tells" how her mother was more sympathetic than she expected, when this really could be the focus of the piece.

I said in part:

The beginning reads just like a story—you take your time setting up the situation—a typical Friday, two friends, etc. You overuse Andi's name a little—once she's in her house alone, you can use "she" almost exclusively, because the reader isn't confused. "Then she begins to get worried." I didn't think you needed the color of the backpack and notebook—usually I ask people to add more details, but those didn't seem to matter a lot. What did add to the mood was the hardness of the kitchen floor where she is sitting as she realizes she left her work at school.

For your revision, I'd like you to try to make this even more vivid—that sinking feeling you get in these situations, her concern that her mother is going to be angry.

Up to this point, I think the essay is basically just fine. What happens next, though, is that you seem to run out of gas. Can't you dramatize—give the actual (or made up) words the mother and daughter say? Also, I think you have an interesting and rather complex thing you learned here—I don't think it is simply that she remembered more than she thought she would; rather, I think it was something about how there are a lot of possibilities for getting out of a problem than a person thinks, or something like that. Anyhow, I'd like you to work a little bit on the "lesson" you learned. . . .

I hope this helps you get back into that essay, which I thought was interesting and you had a hard time with.

Why do you have to get up at 5:30 A.M.? That's awful!

Here is Heather's revision, in which she worked on building suspense and increasing the drama. Her changes are in italics.

"Really? I can't believe she actually said that!" Andi chatted happily with her best friend, Sarah, on the bus *this* afternoon. They had been friends for as long as they could remember, yet they had extremely different *looks* and personalities. Andi was a short brunette, who was usually quiet and shy, while Sarah was tall, blond, outgoing and would often say things that Andi would never dream of saying.

It was a Friday, and although she had a history report due Monday, Andi wasn't the least bit worried about not being able to get it done. After all, she had her notes together, so writing a final copy should take her no more than two hours.

Soon, it was time for her to get off the bus, and, after yelling goodbye to Sarah, Andi started up the long driveway. After letting herself into the house, she grabbed a snack of a brownie and milk and then went into the living room to watch a little bit of MTV. When she had finished eating, *she* decided to get started on her report. She was eager to get it done so that she would be free to do what she wanted for the rest of the weekend.

Andi got up off the couch and walked into the kitchen where she had left her . . . backpack. She looked inside to find her . . . history notebook, where she thought her notes were. After she had flipped through the entire notebook several times and still not found them, Andi decided to look in her textbook. They just have to be here somewhere, she told herself. It wasn't until after she had looked through both her textbook and notebook that she began get*ting* worried. *She emptied out the contents of her bag, and, casting aside her gym clothes, she sat down Indian-style on the floor.* By the time *she* had searched through everything in her book bag, including all of her notebooks, textbooks, and folders, she was in a panic. Her mind raced as she frantically tried to think of where else her notes could be.

Suddenly, Andi jumped up off the hard tile kitchen floor where she had been sitting and stomped into the living room. She flung herself onto the couch, mad at herself for being stupid enough to lose her notes. *She picked up the nearest pillow and threw it across the room, hoping that it would somehow make her less angry. She couldn't believe that she had done all of that work for nothing.* Even if *her notes* were at school, Andi knew that by the time her mother got home it would be locked *anyway.* . . . She was not looking forward to telling her mother that she had forgotten her notes. Andi knew that her mother would not be pleased with her.

As Andi watched her mother come up the driveway she felt as if her life was coming to an end. Her stomach was doing flips, she couldn't remember when she had been this nervous. Her mind raced as she frantically tried to think of how she was going to tell her mother her mistake. She hoped that her mother's lecture wouldn't be too long because she was already disappointed in herself enough. As her mother came through the door Andi took a deep breath and got ready to explain. Several times during Andi's explanation her mother told her either to slow down or not to whine so much, but for the most part she listened quietly. Andi did not think it was going too well, for she could not tell what her mother was thinking by her face. Yet, after she finished her mother was more sympathetic than Andi had envisioned. . . . Her mother *even* offered to type the report as Andi told her the information in the way she wanted it written. *Andi was not surprised, though, when her mother refused to drive her to school.*

Writing her report took longer than Andi first expected, but, considering that she had written it from memory, it hadn't taken very long at all. After that particular incident, Andi always made sure that she was prepared, because, as her mother had taught her, someone wasn't always going to cover for her and make everything right.

In Heather's case, "adding suspense"—which sounds like something only relevant to mystery or horror fiction—deepened the expression of the emotions she felt. This is a case of what teachers of writing—especially teachers of fiction writing—term "show, don't tell." This is one of those old chestnuts that has a lot of truth in it. In most student pieces, writing improves hugely when the generalized telling ("When my dog got lost I felt so bad") is changed to a vivid showing ("When I realized my dog was missing, it was as if somebody had stuck a knife in my stomach"). This can, however, be carried too far: a narrative that describes minutely a character pushing back the comforter, putting his legs over the side of the bed, sticking his feet into his slippers, standing, then slowly walking ten steps to the door, where he turns the knob to the right . . . can get boring, unless this kind of detail has a purpose, comic or otherwise.

In general, if the action is not really vital to the narrative—if it doesn't add some interesting or important or amusing information—then it's usually best to cut it. If your narrative is really about the incredibly embarrassing thing that happened in your first-period class, you can probably skip getting up and cleaning your teeth, and jump-cut (a film term for the times when the scene simply changes abruptly) from the school bus to the classroom, or, perhaps better, start *in medias res*— in the classroom itself. Although I like Heather's second draft, if she were to write a third draft, I would suggest that she summarize the whole beginning, getting rid of Sarah (or better, saving Sarah for a different essay) and starting with "It was a Friday, and although Andi had a history report due Monday. . . ." But as I've mentioned before, it is almost always useful to over-write, then eventually to edit out a great deal of the detail.

TRY THIS: Choose a point in your narrative that seems (to you or your editors and critics) to lack something. Re-imagine the moment and write it in excruciating, overblown detail: turn the doorknob, put in the creak, the weight of the door, the type of doorknob, etc. See if slowing it down gives you time for new ideas to appear.

Another important set of techniques for deepening nonfiction (just as in fiction) is to experiment with new slants, new tones of voice, even different points of view. Students will often start over altogether. This may represent their lack of sophistication about how to go about revision, or it may grow out of an (I hope) outdated assumption that if a teacher wants you to look again at a story or poem or essay, it must be so bad that there is no choice but to start over. Even so, the technique is a useful one. Editors and writers like to use the word *recast* for this, with its connotations of metal being melted down and poured into a new form. It seems to me that the greater the change to a piece, the more opportunity the writer has for new and deeper insights. Obviously, every piece doesn't need to be recast or tried from an entirely fresh aspect, and there is an art to learning when to revise, how much to revise, which pieces to revise, and how long to keep revising.

The following piece of nonfiction writing is an example of a student who, when asked to go back, wrote a new version. A high school student I'll call Maritza, whose first language was not English, wrote this personal narrative:

> I'm going to talk about what happen on my Sweet Fifteen Party. On my sweet fifteen party I was sad because almost like 40 or 50 people went to it. Also I were sad because my mother and my grandmother didn't went to it because they were in the hospital. Because of that I didn't feel good. At the same time that I was sad, I feel happy because my grandfather, best friends, and my boyfriend were with me. They didn't leave me alone. They help me in everything and the way that they were that day make me feel good and proud of them. Before I was leaving my house to go to the church my grandmother call me from the hospital just to tell me God Bless You and I love you. I start crying because my grandmother knew the day of my Sweet Fifteen and my mother didn't.

The second day's assignment was to add more, or make changes in this narrative. Maritza took out a fresh sheet of paper and wrote what was really an entirely new version. I think she must have been in a different mood on the second day. She polished up her English grammar, gave the piece a title, and lightened the tone:

A Sweet Fifteen Party

> It was a sunny and beautiful Saturday. It was on June 9th from last year. That day I were sad because my mother and my grandmother wasn't with me. The cause of that was that both of them were in the hospital.
>
> That day I leave my house to go to the church for the bless. There was a Mazda Club Cars limousine and some of my family. They take me pictures, they help me in everything and it came out pretty.
>
> I celebrated it in a club in Belleville. It was big and pretty, with music and everything, souvenirs, etc.
>
> My cousin nlaw say words for me that day and I pass all that night with the accompany of my boyfriend, family, and best friends.

Maritza's revision is interesting for several reasons. For one thing, she clearly conceives of her second draft as a more formal presentation of the material. She uses a title and paragraphing, and the handwriting is also much neater. Her English verbs are not quite under control yet, but she has made an attempt to regularize them, and the recast second version is altogether a cleaner, easier-to-read paper that is more oriented toward a reader. What also interests me, though, is that she has revised the paper towards an upbeat ending.

In some ways I find the first draft more appealing. On the other hand, while her special day was one of mixed emotions for Maritza, the upbeat ending is the way she wants to memorialize her experience in ink on paper. This would not stop me from suggesting to Maritza that she might consider combining the two versions. I might suggest to her that a piece can end on a happy note but also capture more of the complexity of her feelings that day. I might also suggest that she use the material for several pieces of writing: the happy memory she is working on at first, but also perhaps a separate narrative or a short story about a girl whose sweet fifteen party went badly or ambiguously. The same materials can be used in a number of different ways, and then recombined.

TRY THIS: Write the narrative of some incident from real life that was important to you. A good choice would be a ritual event, such as a wedding, confirmation, bar mitzvah, or graduation. Or you might choose some striking high or low point of your life, such as the first day of school; when you had to have an operation; when your grandmother died; or when your team made the semifinals. Write it once emphasizing funny or unpleasant or ambiguous things that happened, then, at least an hour after finishing the first version, write a second one, putting a different spin on it—emphasize the good if you started with the bad, or the serious side if you emphasized the funny. Then write a combination of the two versions.

TRY THIS: Take the same incident and write a formal essay on the topic—how to make a party a success, or the importance for a child of the first day of school—and use the incident from your real life as a prominent example supporting the thesis of the essay.

To include both the happy and the unhappy is difficult but fruitful both for self-discovery and for capturing some of the complexity of experience. In this way, you can use manipulations of tone and detail in your writing to get a better understanding and control of the experience.

One characteristic of good writers of both fiction and nonfiction is their ability to vary the tone, to come up with different details, ideas, and angles. This allows them to write at different levels, for many purposes.

TRY THIS: Choose a pet peeve of yours—dogs that do their business in your front yard; adults who automatically assume teenagers are up to no good; people who wear sunglasses so you can't see their eyes when they talk to you—whatever. Write a formal letter-to-the-editor on the subject. Then write about it satirically, perhaps in the form of a letter to a close friend who is likely to understand your point of view. Finally, try it as a really down-and-dirty journal entry where you express every bit of anger in you about this particular issue.

TRY THIS: An interesting exercise along these lines is to try talking to yourself in different voices. Do this with a time limit: write criticizing yourself for five minutes, then, when the buzzer sounds, start praising yourself.

Dear Kiki,

You usually throw a fit when your mom or dad tries to correct you. You often torment your sister. You are sometimes lazy. You always worry.

You are pretty responsible. You are good at writing. You are good at art. You love your brother and sister even though you bother them. You have pretty neat handwriting (except when rushing). You are nice most of the time. You did good on the physical fitness test.

—*Kiki Chung, fifth grade*

TRY THIS: Write a true narrative about how some person or thing changed over time. It could be about yourself, another person, a pet, a tree. Then, tell the same story again—from a different point of view. If you tell how you yourself changed, do it once using first person and once using third person.

One of my Expository Writing Tutorial by Mail students, Emily Klinker, did this assignment. Emily came up with two essays about herself, one in her own voice, and one as if told by her older sister. Although I think that both of Emily's essays have a lot of virtues, I don't know which is better. I've used these two essays in teacher workshops as a point of departure for discussion about what kinds of writing we as teachers could encourage.

Emily turned in her essay with a handwritten note that read in part:

The moment I got this assignment in the mail, I was trying to think of something I could write about. It wasn't until about a week ago that I conceived the idea which I ended up writing about. It wasn't until about a week ago that I got [the part about] Karina's hug. The mask is sad but true. I did one day want to cry very badly, but the tears wouldn't come. When I glanced at my reflection as I passed a mirror, I saw that fake grin. . . .

Version I

As a little child I always cried. From breaking something to accidentally coloring out of the lines, the result was always the same; I would cry hysterically. For the longest time, I got sympathy and a much-needed hug whenever I cried. After awhile, however, people began to roll their eyes or disregard me when I started to cry. They were always telling me, "Grow up! You cry too much!"

One day in the second grade was the last straw that it took to break the camel's back. I had been having a particularly rough day, and I finally broke into tears. One of my classmates noticed me crying, and told the teacher; of course the teacher would help. The teacher paused, said that from what she knew, Emily cried very easily, and continued with the lesson. I was simply heartbroken. It seemed like nobody cared about me anymore. I decided that I would show everybody, and resolutely set myself never to cry again.

I cried less and less as weeks turned into months and years. Everytime I broke down and cried, I met with sarcasm and people who just couldn't understand why I would have any reason to cry. This new reason replaced the old childish reason for not crying; if nobody could or would understand, what was the use in crying at all? The only time I ever cried again was when I was alone and could no longer hold back the tears. It was such a rare event that at length I cried only once a year, and sometimes not at all. It seemed like I had been blessed with the face of an angel. My face was always lighted up with a smile, no matter how many tears were flowing in my heart.

It wasn't until I reached Junior High that I realized the full consequence of this face. It had hardened into an unremovable mask, so that in my hour of sorrow, I had only to glance in the mirror to see the mask with its mocking smile, laughing all the more at my distress. So many times I tried to pull the mask away and let my true feelings out, but even my closest friends got only a glimpse. The moment someone asked me if anything was wrong, my mask snapped back into place, and a sweet reply came from the smiling mouth. "Nothing is wrong, I'm just a little tired." I began to hate my own face, wishing its hypocritical smile would vanish and leave me in peace.

Freshman year in high school brought me salvation. I was feeling particularly despondent during a late-night play rehearsal when suddenly I felt myself enveloped in a warm hug. I saw that it was my friend Karina, and asked her why she had given me a hug. "You looked like you needed one." No reply could ever have been more welcome. Someone who cared about me had seen through my garish mask and given me the supporting hug I had needed for four years. As I stood there, I felt a tremendous weight being lifted from my very soul, and I could feel the smiling mask melt away. In its place I found a real smile, one that I have cherished in my heart ever since.

Version II

Emily Klinker was the one child I have known in my life to cry at the drop of a hat. One moment she would be laughing and playing with me, then she would just burst into tears for seemingly no reason. When she was a toddler, I felt sorry for the pudgy little darling, even if I was only one year older, and I'd smother her with hugs and kisses just to bring back that sweet, winning smile. Then she got older and we were all tired of having to soothe good old Emily every other minute; you'd think she would have learned how to deal with problems some other way instead of crying all the time. So instead of taking time out of my busy schedule for the sobbing kid in the corner (I always fancied myself much older than I really was), I'd snap at her and tell her to grow up, or something to that effect. . . . One day after school, I think she was in the second grade at the time, Emily came home sobbing hysterically and wouldn't tell anybody what was wrong. I told her she was probably overreacting and that she was acting like a two-year-old, then turned around and didn't talk to her the rest of the way home. Then Emily began to change. It didn't notice at first, but it seemed like Emily was leading a life that was more charmed every day. She hardly ever cried anymore. Maybe she just learned how to color inside the lines, but soon it was obvious that it was something much bigger than that. By about the middle of her fourth-grade year, I never saw Emily cry again. Even when Pop-pop died, Emily didn't cry. Sure, she was miserable and her face was paler than ever, but I never saw actual tears. That scared me; was there something wrong with my baby sister that I didn't know about? I decided to watch her closely, and that was when I noticed her strange smile. It was always there, always making her look happy; but it stayed there even when she was being yelled at, faintly mocking, and sometimes it looked strained, like Emily wished she was frowning, but the smile was stuck. I wanted to know about that smile, but Emily never mentioned it, and whenever I surprised a faraway look in her eyes, I asked her what was wrong, and the languid answer was always the same: "I'm just tired, that's all." If that was the truth, my sister definitely did not sleep much. Emily had gone without crying for almost four years when I became the proud witness of a sudden, beautiful metamorphosis. We were both in our high school's play that year; I was a sophomore and Emily was a freshman. Emily's smile was very tightly strained when we met after school for play practice. That day, something wonderful happened; Emily and her stuck smile were watching practice from backstage when some other girls and I made our exit from the stage. One of them was Emily's friend Karina, who swept Emily up in a big hug as she danced off the stage. That one spontaneous gesture brought a change to Emily the moment she recovered from her surprise. Emily's face looked like a rose long-encased in ice as the hard shell with its false smile seemed to melt away, leaving in its place an object of genuine beauty; the smile of truth long concealed beneath her mask.

To my taste, the third person story is superior in its details, particularly because of the emergence of the memory of Emily's not crying at her grandfather's funeral. The brusque big-sisterly annoyance with the crying is believable. What is less convincing in the second version, however, is the big sister's offstage observation of what happens between Emily and Karina. Where was she standing to observe this? Behind a convenient curtain? But it is interesting, in both versions, that what breaks out from beneath the mask is also a smile. I wonder if Emily would have let anger break out so easily, or more tears.

The point of this dual essay is not to decide which is better, but to notice what qualities each brings, and—always—to prospect deeper for material. If Emily ultimately decides that the first person is the way to tell the story, she will still have, through her second version, come up with the detail of not crying at her grandfather's funeral.

Essays such as Emily's and Maritza's above offer lots of raw material for other writings: they could be used as examples in a more general or abstract essay, and they would be natural materials for a young adult story or novel. One could imagine Emily writing a story that allows her to express her sorrow again, not just her genuine smile. Such a story could include the sister and Karina as characters, and Emily's teachers and parents; it might make an interesting drama or video play, or a mini-research paper on the meaning of smiles in various cultures or among various individuals.

TRY THIS: Take a personal essay you have written, and try it in another medium: as a drama or poem or short story.

A final type of nonfiction I want to discuss is the interview. Interviews, though factual, often require some editorializing—and in this they have something in common with fiction. Tom Douglass, a scholar and literary interviewer, speaks of arranging material from an interview "in a logical way without losing the relaxed and conversational feel. Interviews are fun to read if you feel that you are there eavesdropping on the person of interest without having to put up with long-winded questions from the interviewer." Douglass further says:

> The main purpose of interviewing has more to do with creating interest rather than scooping hard news, although hard news may come out of an interview. Of course, this idea of creating interest encompasses a wide berth of ethics and taste, ranging from the tawdry tabloid to the exclusively esoteric. Regardless, an interview should showcase the attitudes and ideas of the person being interviewed and not be run roughshod by the interviewer who may have a personal or political desire to put a "spin" on the subject of the interview or the ambition to pull someone's pants down for all the world to see. However, an interview should be an invitation to eavesdrop on conversation that would otherwise not be heard. . . . Human conversation is elliptical, repetitious, and filled with "um's" and "you know's." Even in a highly structured question and answer format, the tendency for spoken language to be understood by nuance and gesture fails to get picked up in a transcribed interview. So in editing and revising interview transcripts, it's important to fill in gaps, supply continuity, and capture the intended meaning of what was being said. For this to be done effectively, it is helpful to keep a journal of impressions and thoughts about the interview. Also, some post-interview fine tuning, some back and forth contact after the interview between the interviewer and the person of interest, is necessary to make sure what was said was intended to be said. . . . However, post-interview contact can also make some problems for revision. There is a tendency to overfix the "um's" and "you know's," to dress the interview up in tuxedo language rather than to keep the conversational and informal quality of blue jeans and sweatshirt language. It is imperative to keep the conversational quality and the eavesdropping feel to an interview. . . . Keep the talk. It is the central appeal of an interview. Keep all of the incomplete sentences and colloquial phrases. Don't let the transcribed spoken language become highly grammatical and formal written language. . . . Conversa-

tion is filled with non-sequitur and rabbit trail examples, and sometimes, these rabbit trails lead to some interesting territory.[2]

Douglass therefore, in revising his interviews, edits out his questions, grouping responses into monologues under large headings such as "On Economics." "Under this large heading," he says, "it is understood that these are the thoughts and attitudes of the person being interviewed. The interviewer is absent from the page. There is no reference to the question asked or to the interviewer. String the monologue together with phrases taken from the questions or unstated assumptions that were mutually understood during the interview."

TRY THIS: Interview a friend, neighbor, teacher, student—anyone you find interesting. Take notes or use a tape recorder, and then transcribe what was said. The next step is to revise the interview, using the guidelines above from Tom Douglass.

The best creative writing—whether fiction, drama, poetry, personal narrative, biography, interview, or any other form—comes out of a process of moving constantly in new directions, deeper directions. Ideally, such writing works through a dialectical process: it is irrational and spontaneous for a while, then rational and planned. You are gripped by some idea or image, which you draft in the heat of inspiration. Later, in the cool light of reason, you cut, reorganize, and add what you perceive to be missing. Then something in what you've written gives you a new idea, and you draft rapidly again, making new connections, perhaps coming up with something you never meant to include. Then you follow with another "rational" session, or show it to another person. Finally, ideally, after many rounds of this process of thesis and antithesis, there is a synthesis, at which point a leap to something that is greater than the sum of its parts becomes possible.

This process doesn't always happen, of course, and often it happens with less than dramatic success. When it does happen, however, the product is the kind of writing that makes a real impact, not only on readers, but on the writer as well.

---

[2] Tom Douglass, in a letter to the author.

PART THREE

◆

SHAPING UP

Chapter Nine

Revising as a Response to Literature

Even in our earliest efforts at writing we are always consciously or unconsciously imitating. We learn to structure our ideas about writing from literary models—the story the teacher read the class or the comic book our big brother gave us. Our first forms are the ones that seem simply to be there. A boy who is engrossed in the origin of superheroes and decides to create his own superhero doesn't agonize over how to begin, any more than I agonize over filling out a subscription coupon: he knows that you start with the superhero's super-characteristics, just as I know what to write in the space labelled "name." In other words, we have conventional structures in our minds even before we read and write, and conventional structures are often exactly what is needed. Thus one thing a teacher can give students is familiarity with and practice in such forms. This can be done only through wide reading and lots of practice.

"Conventional" structures and "creative" writing are by no means antithetical. I love the fresh, the new, and the original, but making a fetish of it is a twentieth-century quirk. In the sixteenth century, mastery of the conventions of sonnet writing was a desirable accomplishment. Variations were of course necessary, but the main project was to master the form with its exact number of lines, its set rhyme scheme, and the tropes that were appropriate to it—just the way a great basketball player does not make up the art of dribbling, but embellishes and perfects it.

My son Joel was assigned his first homework composition in the late winter of first grade. The assignment was to write something about the season, and he sat down and rapidly wrote a little half-poem half-essay about snow and children sliding and sledding. Not only did the piece sound nothing like his speaking voice, but we had not even had any snow yet. My satisfaction was in the beginning of his mastery of forms and levels of discourse. It was his idea of what he thought appropriate for a seasonal composition, his maiden voyage on the ocean of formal writing.

Some of my own earliest efforts at writing were imitations of popular culture. In chapter two I quoted a poem I wrote about Fredy the Cowboy, which was essentially a commercial jingle. I turned to the funny papers and comic books for my models, because those were my first forms of literature. I carefully drew blocks, made pictures, squeezed words into the balloons—and one day discovered that if you write the words first and make the speech balloon afterwards, you don't have to squeeze. This was a technical breakthrough—the beginning of my taking control of conventions and forms.

As I got older, I would write my own version of whatever I read or saw: after the movie version of *Old Yeller,* I wrote a story called "The Yaller Dog." My version was not plagiarized, but something much less civilized: I wanted to get inside the story and eat it from the inside, like a voracious little larva working its way out of a fruit. In my version of the dog story, the dog doesn't die at the end. This doesn't mean that I hated the original or was traumatized by it, only that I wanted to do it my way.

One theory of literature states that what is written is only fully realized when a reader receives it, that the reader is, in a way, the true creator of a text; a poem or essay or novel or news article does not really exist until the reader has filled in the gaps with his or her own experience and knowledge. The psychology of the author and the author's intentions are nothing compared to the activity of the reader, who by recognizing conventions and transforming them with his or her own perceptions and beliefs creates what *is* on the page through the activity of reading it. As one theorist says, "The whole point of reading . . . is that it brings us into deeper self-consciousness, catalyzes a more critical view of our own identities."[1]

While I don't embrace this theory entirely, I am struck by the idea that a textbook, a story, a poem, a newspaper article, or a magazine essay is not something to be treated with exaggerated respect. This idea is of enormous practical value for those of us who teach.

---

[1] Wolfgang Iser, as quoted by Terry Eagleton in *Literary Theory: An Introduction* (Minneapolis: Univ. of Minnesota Press, 1983), p. 79.

TRY THIS: The next time you read something leisurely—the sports page, *TV Guide,* or an article in *People* magazine—write a quick response to your reading. Include whatever is on your mind, even if it doesn't seem to be on the subject. Write about how hot the weather is, or your concerns for your team's standing in the league, or whatever. Do this over a few days with the same type of reading material.

When you have three or more entries, revise them into an essay in the form of a feature article or review, such as an essay on Ann Landers or this season's Cleveland Indians.

Writing can thus be a way of making what you read your own and altering what you read to make it fit yourself. Some years ago, I was teaching a required first-year literature course at Pace University. For many of the students, this would be the final go-round with the standard English literary canon, and—to add insult to injury—this class met on Friday afternoons. We had some good times in that class, although attendance was always sporadic. When we came to the required grappling with *Hamlet,* a number of the students were willing to try anything rather than actually read the text, and when they did read it, they seemed at a loss as to how to talk about it. I typed up some of the more famous monologues ("How all occasions do inform against me . . ." and "O, my offense is rank, it smells to heaven!") for closer study, and then asked everyone to choose a character in the play (excluding Hamlet himself) and write a prose or poetic monologue. To my surprise, several students tried something in blank verse, and most had a better grasp of the character they chose than I would have expected. Overall, I felt each of the students was able to think better—and consequently learned more—about the play through the revision exercise than they would have in class discussion alone. To speak analytically about literature requires a kind of training that these students had not had and might never have, but writing these pieces allowed them to meet the literature on their own terms, and showed me that they really did understand the play.

TRY THIS: If your class is studying *Hamlet* (or some other famous work), have each of them write a dramatic monologue for a minor character. This exercise helps students learn how to imitate a form (the dramatic monologue) and to revise the text by imagining its events from a different point of view.

I, Laertes, despise the wretched Hamlet.
Such a fool as he deserves no kingship.
No true king would allow the transparency
of marriage to obstruct divine ascending
to the crown as did Claudius to Hamlet.
His soul is a flicker where mine flares.
That king fool we have now
who thinks from his groin
would never have eliminated his predecessor
were it not for my connivance.
Yet I still have no power;
I'll seek Fortinbras in this matter.
Now with my father dead,
his spirit rises with opportunity;
opportunity in the guise of revenge.
To kill Hamlet with the poison sword
Claudius shall give me!
Upon Hamlet's death, there shall be great mourning,
a nation in distress.
It is then that I shall expose
Claudius and his foul plans.
Revolutionary upheaval will follow,
and a divided Denmark will surrender
to Fortinbras' invading armies,
and I shall have power.

—*Tom Wright, first-year college student*

* * * * *

Claudius

I am now dying—and what for I ask. Here I have the throne and a beautiful queen. I have power throughout the land and am very happy. Why must I die by the sword of such a brash young prince? Life has finally been good to me, till now.

True, I have deeply sinned. I killed, manipulated, and schemed to get to the top. If only I could have done away with Hamlet sooner. I knew that crazy fit by Hamlet was an act. He always suspected me of killing his father.

It is so sad it has to end this way. I was just getting used to the idea of being the one with unchecked power and the final say in stately matters. It is a shame that I was outwitted by such a young prince like

Hamlet. And yet he dies too. Now that is indeed sweet revenge. All I can say is, at least I made it to the top.

—*Wayne Hugar, first-year college student*

TRY THIS: If your students are studying a particular period in history, find a poem or two written at the time, and have students pretend to be the poet and write another poem about some other event or theme of the day, imitating the form and style. You can try the same thing using a news article from the actual period, a short story, or—perhaps best of all—a journal entry or letter.

Writing your way into literature by making your own versions can include both direct imitations (such as the Shakespearean dramatic monologue) and more playful exercises (such as writing anachronistic news reports about the events surrounding Hamlet's death). In both kinds of writing, the student changes the existing literature in order to get closer to it, deeper inside it. This approach to studying literature works as well with modern literature as with older literature. Monologues are particularly good for getting inside characters. I asked my college students to write pieces based on "Cutting Edge," a story by James Purdy about an unpleasant confrontation in a family when a son comes home with a beard and his mother wants him to shave it.[2] One student wrote his piece from the young man's point of view:

She is so blind. She can't possibly see beyond this beard.

I know that trying to change our damaged relationship is not likely but I want her to accept me as who I am and start building our relationship.

I am a new man now and unless you accept me and the things that are in the present, we won't get anywhere. I can't believe that she will refuse to accept the past.

What do you think of my face that's naked in its raw form? This beard is clothes for my face. What do you want? Nude? Or clothed?

There's no hope. We are finished as a family. I don't want to see you again. It's quite clear that you don't want to see me.

—*Jae Song, college junior*

---

[2] Reprinted in Janet Burroway, *Writing Fiction: A Guide to Narrative Craft*, 2nd ed. (Glenview, Ill.: Scott, Foresman, and Company, 1987).

These next examples were written by high school students. I had them read one of my short stories, "Evenings With Porter."[3] The story is about two characters who meet at various points in their lives. The male character is about to go overseas as a pilot in the Vietnam War, and the female narrator tries to convince him not to. I then had the students rewrite one of the scenes from the male character's point of view:

> Just came back from Blair Ellen's Grandmother's store. I was there for a long while. Hangin' out and drinkin' pop. I went this afternoon. It's now past dark. I remember walkin' in to the store. Blair Ellen sold me a pop. She looked kind of cute, I mean for 12. After my pop, I hang around a little longer, we, Blair Ellen and me, went out on the porch to talk. We talked of the town boys and such. After a bit, her grandmother was rustlin' about the kitchen makin' noise. I guess Blair Ellen had chores to do or had to attend to her grandmother 'cause she said good night and left. We cut our talkin' kinda short. I'll prob'ly go back tomorrow.
>
> —*Kate Renlow, tenth grade*

*   *   *   *   *

> Now, I'm flying all alone, I'm fighting for my country. I'm very scared, even though I told her I wasn't. I wish I would of listened to her, and flew up into Canada. Why can't I just turn around now, and go back and be with her? Well, I gave my devotion to the Air Force and this is where I'm going to stay. I just hope I'll stay alive, so when this is over, I can see her again. Now as I reach Cambodia, I'm even more scared, but I'll be alright, won't I. . . .
>
> —*Rick Raymond, tenth grade*

The thing that pleased me about this exercise was how much in tune the students seemed to be with the story. They chose to go into it at various points, but in each case I found myself believing their interpretation. This piece also reaffirmed my sense that often a so-called creative or reader-involved response is the best one to literature for non-specialized students. When the student can take something he or she is reading and revise it, there is likely to be much

---

[3] Meredith Sue Willis, "Evenings with Porter," *Pikeville Review* (Humanities Department, Pikeville College, Pikeville, KY 41501), Spring, 1988.

more real understanding of its shape and texture. I am certainly not suggesting that there should never be critical writing about literature, but that critical writing should be only one of several ways of engaging students in literature. Personal involvement through revising literature should always precede critical thinking, because it is extremely difficult to think deeply about a work of art with which you have never really been connected.

TRY THIS: After reading any story or novel (preferably one in the first person), write one scene from the point of view of a character other than the narrator. Do this by assigning parts before the class begins reading the novel so that each class member has one character to follow and study throughout the work.

One quick way of using an author's writing to get a feel for its shape is through copying and dictation. I am always collecting samples of fiction to use with students and in my articles and books on writing, and I have typed many paragraphs by my favorite authors, poets and nonfiction writers as well as novelists and short story writers. It's a great feeling to have someone else's words go through your body—learning what the rhythm of those words feels like, the shape of the paragraphs or the length of the lines. Imitating and copying should be, it seems to me, among our regular language arts activities.

TRY THIS: Find some poem or paragraph that you admire and copy it longhand. If you are a teacher, bring in a piece that you admire and ask students to copy it over. This can be followed by the writing of an imitation or a continuation.

TRY THIS: Try the same exercise through dictation, having someone read aloud while the rest write it down.

TRY THIS: Do this with a poem, and then compare how you broke the lines with how the poet did it.

TRY THIS: After using copying or dictation, turn the paper over and, without looking, write down as much of it as you can remember. Compare the two pieces. Do you like your own remembered version better? Try writing it again a week later. The point is not to get a headache trying to remember, but to see what your memory adds and changes.

TRY THIS: Type a sonnet or other fairly compact poem, or a dense paragraph of prose, leaving out most of the middle, keeping just the first and last lines, or sentences, or perhaps the final rhyme scheme if it's a sonnet. Duplicate and distribute, and have everyone fill it in with their own versions. Depending on the students' ages and your own style, you can do this either by requiring the poem to be completed with the exact number of lines as the original poem (as in the example below) or by letting the middle part be as long or short as the students want.

> Over my head, I see the bronze butterfly,
> Asleep on the black trunk,
>
> _____
> _____
> _____
> _____
> _____
> _____
> _____
> _____
> _____
>
> I have wasted my life.[4]

TRY THIS: Pass out the opening paragraph or line of some famous prose work, and have everyone continue the story. For some real fun, see what younger students can do with "Call me Ishmael" or "It was the best of times, it was the worst of times."

TRY THIS: Instead of starting with the words, give the plot of some famous story: married woman falls in love with other man, destroys her marriage, in despair kills herself. (That's Tolstoy's _Anna Karenina_.) Flesh it out.

---

[4] These three lines are from James Wright's "Lying in a Hammock at William Duffy's Farm in Pine Island, Minnesota." For the full text of the poem, see appendix.

Kids imitate whether you want them to or not—in fact, we all do, in life and in writing. For me, writing comes out of the experience of daily life (including all our language and mental imagery) and from literature. For many students, of course, literature (and much life experience) has been replaced by television and, to a lesser extent, the movies. It seems to me only fair and realistic to make a space for imitating models the students already have and are comfortable with. Thus student writers should get a turn at writing music lyrics or television scripts. Of course, there is a job of analysis here too—to understand the forms that are used by professional songwriters and television writers.

I observed writer-in-the-schools Josefina Baez working with eighth grade students at the Bergen Street School in Newark, New Jersey. The class was a small group of eighth graders, and Josefina perched on a desk, with the students arranged in a horseshoe open to the blackboard. The classroom teacher was sitting at her own desk. Josefina used the students' own choice, rap poetry, as a means of working through the process of revision. The poems sprang from the students' ideas and themes, which included drugs, pollution, and getting a paycheck versus getting a welfare check. The students first wrote their verses—which they discovered took more effort than they expected—then they transcribed the lyrics to the blackboard one at a time. Everyone helped ensure that the mechanics were right. After making written revisions on the board, the students then read the poems aloud in various styles: as sentences; as poetry; as rhythmic rap. One boy said, "Hey, mine could be a slow song, too," and proceeded to sing it, and the teacher said, "Why, that could be blues—" and then *she* took a turn singing the student's lines. It was a great atmosphere for showing how words can be changed and exchanged.

After this group session, the rap poems were revised individually by the students, typed up by Josefina, and prepared both for performance and for inclusion in a written anthology. Josefina's students learned a number of things simultaneously: how they can use one another's critiques to make changes, as well as individual revising and editing under the supervision of adults; that their poems can cross into other media—printed in a booklet and performed for an audience; and that songs do not appear magically in a music video. Much work precedes even a popular form.

TRY THIS: Have your students choose any song form that they like. Depending on geographic location and when you are reading this book, you might get country music, rap, heavy metal, or something I've never heard of. What is essential here is that the students choose *their* music, whatever it is. Have them transcribe lyrics, and then write their own, using the form as you've analyzed it from the songs they bring in. Next, discuss how accurately the pieces followed the form, and how to make them better.

TRY THIS: Try the same thing but with a television or movie script. Again, decide together what the elements of a television drama or, say, a horror movie are.

TRY THIS: Choose a poem or song that you like and ask everyone to write an imitation of it. Have the students write before any discussion, so that they can discover the elements and form on their own. (Later, when they discuss the poem and compare their imititations, they will pick up more elements and figure out more about the form.) After one draft of writing, read aloud, discuss what people chose to imitate, and then have them do a second draft, giving everyone the opportunity to imitate further, or add further elements or stylistic devices. There are a number of excellent poems that lend themselves to imitation by many different ages of children. Look through any good anthology for poems that appeal to you.[5] There are many forms to try, including calligrams, visual poems that imitate the shapes of the things they are about.

Revising previous works of literature is another approach to writing fiction. For example, some years ago I read the *Confessions* of Saint Augustine in conjunction with a biography of him. Augustine mentions his concubine of many years—mother of his son—but never tells her name. I had many reactions to reading Augustine and learned a great deal, but this particular fact stuck in my craw, and I wrote a short story called "Sermon of the Younger Monica," which was from the concubine's point of view. This was a deeply satisfying exercise for me, as were other stories I wrote, including a

---

[5] One particularly useful anthology of contemporary poems by adults and children is *The Poetry Connection* by Kinereth Gensler and Nina Nyhart (New York: Teachers & Writers, 1978).

revision of Shakespeare and a couple of Biblical revisions. In my version of the Adam and Eve story, I embedded sentences from the King James translation of the Bible as well as a fragment of Milton's description of the serpent in *Paradise Lost.*

Revisionist literature has a very long and venerable tradition: Aeschylus's *Oresteia* uses material from Homer, who borrowed from previous stories of the gods and heroes. Eugene O'Neill wrote his own version of the same material in *Mourning Becomes Electra.* Parodies and travesties are time-honored literary forms, and science fiction includes a whole sub-genre of writing about what would have happened if history had been changed. A few years ago, a science fiction editor solicited stories that answered the question, "What if, at each presidential election in the history of the United States, there had been a different outcome?" What would have happened if Lincoln had lost his election? If Richard Nixon had become president in 1960 instead of in 1968? Judy Moffett wrote a story that had Davy Crockett defeat Andrew Jackson with positive results for the United States government's policies toward Native Americans. Beryl Bainbridge has a mainstream novel called *Young Adolf* about a visit Adolf Hitler may or may not have paid to England in his adolescence, when his brother lived there, and Leon Rooke's novel *Shakespeare's Dog* revises history from the canine point of view.

TRY THIS: Write a poem or story from the point of view of some minor character in literature—someone whose life was affected by the hero, but who did not necessarily see things the way the hero did. This can shed new light on the story, perhaps from a comic point of view.

TRY THIS: Try writing an imitation of some brief passage or short work, such as a parable. Write it in such a way that you critique the original or give a different emphasis.

This parable from Franz Kafka is followed by a high school student's revision of it:

A Little Fable

"Alas," said the mouse, "the world is growing smaller every day. At the beginning it was so big that I was afraid, I kept running and running, and I was glad when at last I saw walls far away to the right and left, but these long walls have narrowed so quickly that I am in the last chamber already, and there in the corner stands the trap that I must run into." "You only need to change your direction," said the cat, and ate up the mouse.

—*Franz Kafka*[6]

*   *   *   *   *

"Help!" the mouse yelled. He stood caught in the trap and had no means of escape. "Surely," he thought, "one of my many friends will rescue me before The Cat comes." He waited and waited and yelled and yelled, yet no one came. Finally, he saw a mouse running to him. "Mother!" he yelled. "You could be killed. The Cat will surely be here any minute! Please, save yourself and allow one of my many friends to save me," he pleaded.

"No, I will save you my son," she said.

"But mother, why is it none of my friends came?" the little mouse asked.

"Son, it is true, you have many friends and you have chosen them well, but only one is your mother," she said as they ran together back into the wall, just as The Cat lunged for them.

—*Billy Maris, tenth grade*

Billy captures the style very well, but revises the ending to fit his own world view. This "answering back" to literature and other arts is one of the things that writers do all the time. Filmmakers use showers and towers and crowds of birds and dozens of other images that allude to Alfred Hitchcock; Anthony Hecht revises Matthew Arnold's "Dover Beach" in a humorous poem called "Dover Bitch."

TRY THIS: Do a modern version of some other parable or fable. Aesop's are good models, as are the parables of Jesus.

TRY THIS: Write your own Zen parable, using the brief, surprising forms that the Zen masters use to make their students think in new ways.

---

[6] As translated by Willa and Edwin Muir in Franz Kafka, *The Complete Stories of Franz Kafka* (New York: Schocken Books, 1971).

Learning to Be Silent

The pupils of the Tendai school used to study meditation before Zen entered Japan. Four of them who were intimate friends promised one another to observe seven days of silence.

On the first day all were silent. Their meditation had begun auspiciously, but when night came and the oil lamps were growing dim one of the pupils could not help exclaiming to a servant: "Fix those lamps."

The second pupil was surprised to hear the first one talk. "We are not supposed to say a word," he remarked.

"You two are stupid. Why did you talk?" asked the third.

"Ha! I am the only one who has not talked!" concluded the fourth pupil.[7]

This process of using existing literature to form your own literature can be done directly, through imitation, or through the answering back of parody and rewriting, and also through something I call embedding. Embedding consists of incorporating a previous piece in a new work. One particular embedding exercise is one of my all-time favorites. It works at many levels of age and competency. I especially like to do it once with total open-endedness, then have a discussion and send students back to have another go at it. Notice that this is not a beginning but a fragment of dialogue with a possible conflict in it.

TRY THIS: Here is a Skeleton Story. Copy these words on your paper with at least three spaces between each line.

Hi.

Hi.

Where were you?

Nowhere.

Take these words and do anything you want to them to make the story longer and more interesting. Add, change, reverse, cut. (See the dialogue exercise in chapter seven that starts with a scrap of real life dialogue and turns it into fiction.)

---

[7] Paul Reps, *Zen Flesh, Zen Bones* (Rutland, Vt.: Charles E. Tuttle, Co., 1957). See appendix for more Zen parables.

"Hi," said Jessie, her blonde hair bouncing up and down.

"Hi, it's nice to see you again," said Samantha, struggling to hold her duffel bag.

"Where were you?" Jessie wondered, eyeing her duffel bag suspiciously.

"Nowhere," said Samantha, thinking how nosy her friend was being.

"Well, you had to be somewhere if you weren't home last night when I called!" she said, anger sparkling in her wide blue eyes.

"You don't have to know everywhere I go," said Samantha, thinking about how much fun she had last night when she slept over at Kelly's house.

"Well, then, good-bye," said Jessie, stomping off gruffly.

—Erika Robinson, sixth grade

After everyone writes for five or ten minutes, have a short discussion and read a few pieces, to show different ways the students handled the assignment. You might brainstorm a list of ways people made their boring conversation interesting: by adding gestures, narration, and setting; describing people, specifying tone of voice, etc.

TRY THIS: Do the same exercise, requiring that everyone write for at least ten minutes (or whatever length you choose). This generates more details.

TRY THIS: Go out on the street or to some public place and collect fragments of dialogue. Bring them back and write up just the words, then try to reconstruct a whole scene from memory.[8]

TRY THIS: Do the same thing, by making up the scene, rather than by remembering it.

TRY THIS: Do the same thing, but exchange skeletons with someone who wasn't in your group so that everyone has a bit of dialogue to use that is new to them.

In one of my novels, I wrote a scene that I realized was very much like a particular Kafka parable. I tried typing and embedding

---

[8] See chapter seven.

Kafka's words as a focus for my visualization of the moment of crisis in my novel. Kafka's parable "The Vulture" ends with:

> Falling back, I was relieved to feel him drowning irretrievably in my blood, which was filling every depth, flooding every shore.[9]

My scene ends as follows:

> She laid her hands on her thighs and stared at her fate, at the embodied shriek that plunged and plunged, plunged deep into her throat. She felt it fill her depths, flood her shores.

I should note here that this is not plagiarism because the original material is altered so much, and also because I am not trying to pass off an entire work by someone else as my own. Jane Wilson Joyce does something along these same lines but much more extensively in her beautiful poem-saga of the Oregon Trail, *Beyond the Blue Mountains*.[10] She uses passages of diary entries of real individuals who went on the Oregon Trail in their covered wagons, and reorganizes and embeds those bits of diaries and journals in her narrative poem, hangs her work on these structuring elements, these bones of found language. Here is one poem from her book:

> Not a tree,
> not a stone,
> nothing
> but flowers and grass.
> We women
> spread our skirts
> for one another,
> spread them wide as if about to
> curtsey, plain
> wool and figured
> calico, overlapped,
> a courtly dance of
> modesty.[11]

She is able to pinpoint her sources for this poem: all from *Women's Diaries of the Westward Journey*: "Not a drop of water, nor a spear of grass to be seen, nothing but barren hills, bare and broken

---

9 For the full text, see appendix.
10 Jane Wilson Joyce, *Beyond the Blue Mountains* (Frankfort, Ky.: Gnomon Press, 1992).
11 Ibid., p. 26.

rock, sand and dust" (p. 207) and "Passed what is called the fort, chimney & other bluffs, in appearance resembling castles, capitals of cities" (p. 65), along with introductory material about women's need of each other for keeping their modesty while attending to bodily functions.[12] She describes the process of putting together her book:

> Looking back at the process [of writing *In the Blue Mountains*] now, I'd say there are probably five basic methods:
>   1. Straight found poems (ex. "Oh my dear Mother")
>   2. Pastiche found poems (ex. "Pressing On")
>   3. Photo-based poems (ex. "A company of emigrants")
>   4. Incident-based poems (ex. "Accident")
>   5. Free inventions (ex."We passed a rosewood/spinet")
> There are mixed methods within poems, too. The main thing is that I immersed myself in Lillian Schlissel's book. There was a time when I could lay my hand on any phrase in its 200+ pages. . . . Another hidden resource is, of course, my personal stock of memories and experiences and impressions.[13]

TRY THIS: Take a journal or letter of your own, or perhaps better, of your parents or some ancestor, and choose phrases that move you. Use these as structures for a piece of prose or poetry, fiction or nonfiction. Let them form the posts you hang other material on.[14]

TRY THIS: Copy a poem, preferably one from previous centuries or otherwise difficult, then write your own paragraph, short essay, dramatic scene, anecdote, or whatever you want based on that poem. Change it as far as you'd like, perhaps in the end leaving no more than a few choice verbs.

Consciously, unconsciously, and self-consciously, we are always using previous literature when we write: we imitate what went before us; we sometimes react against it; once in a while we make something genuinely new of it.

---

[12] *Women's Diaries of the Westward Journey,* ed. Lillian Schlissel (New York: Schocken Books, 1982).
[13] Jane Wilson Joyce in a private letter to the author.
[14] See also William Carlos Williams's long poem *Paterson* (New York: New Directions, 1963), which incorporates previously existing material.

Chapter Ten
Beginning and Polishing

One of the recurring themes of this book is the close intertwining of drafting, revision, and polishing. More than once, when I thought I was in the final polishing stages of these chapters, I found myself plunging again into deep revision. This chapter on finishing is therefore not the final chapter: the last chapter will go into the quintessentially deep revision of shaping and structuring, especially long works. This next-to-last chapter is about techniques for revising a piece of writing in order to communicate more effectively with its reader through good beginnings and certain kinds of polishing.

Beginnings as Process, Beginnings as Product

The first few pages of a book are of great importance, but they probably aren't what the writer wrote first. Recognizing this can be enormously liberating: you don't have to come up with a Great Opening Line before you can begin to write.

When my first novel was accepted for publication, I was teaching writing at P.S. 75 in Manhattan, and I was so stunned by my good fortune that I stopped people I hardly knew to tell them the good news, including some third graders I ran into in the hall.

"Guess what!" I told them. "I have a book that's going to be published!"

One of them said, "You mean like a book?"

"Yes!" I said. "Exactly like a book, with a cover, and you'll be able to buy it in a store!"

"Oh wow!" they said. "What's the name of it?"

"Well," I said, "I have some changes to make, and the editor wants me to work on a name."

"It doesn't have a name yet?" said one little girl, looking skeptical.

"I'm still thinking about the name."

The three kids exchanged looks, and the skeptical girl said, "You're joking. You didn't really write a book!"

And it took me a long while to convince them that I had actually written a book that didn't have a name yet. It was strongly fixed in their minds that you sit down and write a title, an author's name, then the first line, then the second, and so on through the body of the work until finally you inscribe THE END and are finished.

Even adult writers often believe that you have to get the beginning right before you can go on. Indeed, polishing the beginning until you have figured out where to go next *is* one time-honored technique for revising, but it is a technique that causes many people to get stuck. Another technique, equally venerable, is to skip the beginning altogether until you know your work well enough to be clear about how you want a reader introduced to it.

From the point of view of revision, then, we are actually talking about two different things when we talk about beginnings. One is how you get yourself started in your work, and one is deciding what the reader should read first. When people say of a book, "That's my kind of story: it has a beginning and a middle and an end," they usually mean that they are comfortable with the piece, that its shape is familiar and recognizable—that it is, to use computer jargon, user-friendly. But even if the work in question is a difficult or demanding one, it always has a beginning in the sense that the reader enters the work at some point.

When I am writing a short nonfiction piece with a deadline, such as a book review, the beginning the reader reads is often where I actually *did* start. I revise the beginning early on and go through many versions almost immediately. The beginning can be a shorthand way of settling on style and approach. If I don't have a beginning that seems to contain my whole idea in a nutshell, I revise it, and use the process of revision to organize my thoughts. I know that when I have finally solved the beginning, I will have unlocked the door to the direction the whole piece will take.

With a longer piece, however—particularly fiction, but often in nonfiction too—my process of beginning often results in a lot of writing that I come back to and cut before showing it to anyone else. The opening is more like a sketch—something for me, not the reader. Thus in writing a long work, I may draft the beginning rapidly, knowing that it will probably be changed, and plunge forward. Sometimes I don't even write a beginning at all, but go directly to the middle and draft whatever scenes grip me most. Often I settle on the beginning only *at the very end*, after I have drafted and revised two or three times. In the book you are reading now, for example, it wasn't until the final weeks of revising that I decided which material to use as chapter one. What you read as the opening came out of the process of editing and finishing. Finding a good lead or beginning for a piece is one essential part of the final polishing.

One of my Expository Writing Tutorial students wrote:

> Of all the things I could describe, I might as well tell about one to which I can relate. As I maybe have said in one of my letters or assignments, I am an intense video game player. Whenever I can, I am in my room blasting monsters or sacking a quarterback. My friend Ronnie also has this "videogame-itis": as my father loves to call it. . . .
>
> —*Brian Weinthal, eighth grade*

I wrote back to him:

> The present opening is very informal—probably too informal. You say, "Of all the things I could describe, I might as well tell about one to which I can relate." It strikes me that this is you thinking aloud, as it were, or talking to me, the teacher, or just warming up. I always do this on the computer or typewriter when I start to write—I think aloud, wander around, remind myself of my purpose—and then, I usually find a real beginning and cut the informal stuff at the beginning. In my opinion, your real beginning would be more powerful if you started right in with "I am an intense video game player. Whenever I can, I am in my room blasting monsters or sacking a quarterback."

Jen Colaguori (another EWT student) began a personal narrative essay called ". . . But the Memories Live On" this way:

> I ascended the steps of the Greyhound bus, prepared for the best summer of my life.
>
> I took a seat next to my friend, and we exchanged glances of excitement. I looked out the window, and as soon as I waved good-bye to my parents, I was ready for camp spirit.
>
> This would be my third year at overnight camp in the Poconos.

*   *   *   *   *

> Before I knew it, two short months had flown by, and I was back on the bus, but, this time, I was headed home. . . .

When I read this piece, it seemed to me that the whole first section had more to do with Jen's process of figuring out how to tell the story—where to begin it—than with the story itself, whose subject is the events that take place at home. Some of what happened (the death of a pet) took place while she was at camp, but the focus of the narrative is not on camp, where she knew nothing about the pet's illness, but on what happened when she got home. What is important in the piece is that she was at camp, not how she set off or who was her seat partner. Not for this essay, at any rate. Her writing about all that was important to her process of reconstructing that particular summer, but far less important to the reader.

In the margin, I wrote, "This doesn't seem to go anywhere—I'd start with the return from camp," and Jen, always alert to suggestions, edited her essay so that it begins simply:

> Before I knew it, two short months had flown by, and I was back on the bus headed home. My third summer at camp was great! My heart was pounding, because I was so excited to see my parents and Kippy, my miniature schnauzer. . . .

For beginning writers, the use of chatty, everyday language (even direct address to a listener, as in Brian's piece above) is an important step, but students such as Brian and Jen are ready to learn the difference between the process of drafting and the finished product.

Some good tricks for leading into a personal essay such as Jen's or Brian's are: (1 start with a question; (2 start with a vivid detail or quotation; (3 start with a little story; (4 start with something funny. Nonfiction writers frequently begin with an anecdote or a passage of narrative or description that uses fiction techniques to create a sense of immediacy. Often, if the first lines intrigue the readers enough, they will read the rest of the essay, no matter how difficult it is.

TRY THIS: Write several different "leads" or catchy beginnings to a piece you're working on. Try a question, a joke, an anecdote, a vivid description, or something in the present tense. Here are two examples:

> Who killed Christopher Robin? This is the question readers of *Winnie-the-Pooh* have been asking themselves ever since the terrible fate of. . . .

> The scene of the crime is deceptively bucolic: ancient oak trees abound, but the sense of something amiss is brought home by the broken jar of honey and the swarm of flies that circle it. . . .

After you've written several leads, ask a friend, teacher, or family member to read them. Ask them which one would make them want to read more.

Original version

This story happened in the summer going into 1989. My family went to New York for a little vacation. We visited my uncle, some stores, some popular sights, some friends' houses, and a house my uncle was working on.

Revised version

Have you ever done something so stupid that when you think about it, you wonder how you could be that stupid? My story begins in Bayside, New York, during the summer of 1988. My family and I went there for a mini-vacation.

—*John Chung, ninth grade*

TRY THIS: Take the several beginnings you have written, and try them out on more people—at least three, *of various ages.* Make it a survey. Which beginnings appeal to people your own age? Older? To younger kids? Which age group are you writing for? Would you consider writing two different versions, for readers of different ages? And for whom are you writing anyhow? For your teacher? For your Uncle Zhores? For your best friend? What if no one likes the first sentence *you* like? Are you writing for other people, or yourself?

TRY THIS: Try to come up with the most boring or clichéd beginning you can. "It was a dark and stormy night. . . ." Do this as a competition with a friend, and find some friends to vote on whose is worse.

TRY THIS: How many beginnings of novels or poems can you and your friends recall by memory? "All happy families are alike but an unhappy family is unhappy after its own fashion." "It was the best of times, it was the worst of times." This is an exercise in analyzing how a finished work does its job.

TRY THIS: Draft rapidly five first sentences—they may be beginnings for stories or articles you have always wanted to write, or just some ideas that come to you. Which ones seem to work best? Are there any of them you might continue to work on?

TRY THIS: Take a piece you have written or an idea you have (a place you've been, an event you witnessed), and write a couple of sentences of it as a beginning six different ways, as if you were opening:

a personal essay (nonfiction)
a poem
a letter to a friend
a novel
a short story
a feature article for a newspaper.

Cutting, Polishing, and Critiquing

I don't believe there is always only one right way of saying something. There are certain short poems of Emily Dickinson's that seem perfect to me—particularly some of her revisions made years after the first draft[1]—but often the best way to convey an idea or feeling varies with the writing situation. For example, you often edit out a really terrific word or image and replace it with a more ordinary one because it seems to draw too much attention to itself and slows down the reader. Other times, of course, you do the opposite: you come up with a word that really is a show stopper, because at that moment you know the show should be stopped.

For me, the cutting, polishing, and critiquing are both hard work and great pleasure. It is the time when you step back from your work and narrow your eye at it to make sure it is presenting its best side. But polishing can also be a time for final insights into the material, particularly in poetry writing.

I observed poet/performance artist Kurtis Lamkin doing a one-day poetry workshop with eighth graders in Newark, New Jersey. He was talking about imagery. "For our purposes," he said, "an image is a word picture, but also something you can see and touch." His assignment was to take the phrase "My soul is a—" and find an image for one's own soul. The second line was to be "My soul (does something)."

What interested me about his lesson was that the assignment itself was only the merest beginning. The real lesson was in plunging

---

[1] See the exercise at the end of this chapter.

into cutting and polishing as a way of doing deep poetry revision on the spot. One of Kurtis's techniques was to write his own poem in front of the class, as they were writing theirs. He wrote on the board:

My soul is a falcon
It dreams under a cliff

When everyone had written two lines, he said, "Now we're really going to start. Let the first line be your first line and the second line be your *last* line, and put three more lines in between."

My soul is a falcon

_____

_____

_____

It dreams under a cliff

The class wrote enthusiastically, and while not everyone precisely followed the instructions, Khalilah Knight did. She had first written:

My soul is a parrot
It talks every day

Then she expanded the poem to:

My soul is a parrot.
It sleeps in a cage.
It devours food and sips water.
It fly around in its cage by itself.
It talks in a coughing voice.

Khalilah revised her last line as she was working, just as Kurtis did. As he was showing the students how to fill in the blanks, he had said, "Well, I think I'll just change this other line while I'm here— it's been bothering me," so everyone knew that the point was to follow your vision, not the directions.

The next part of the assignment involved some serious cutting. Kurtis asked everyone to go through the poem and cut out the "My soul is" and all the "it's," and to make the first image the title. As he continued to tinker with his own poem in front of the class, he made more cuts and changes. His piece came out as:

The Falcon

Wakes the morning with a shriek
Clutches the river's first splash
Lifts like dust
Dreams under a cliff.

Khalilah's next draft was:

Parakeet

Sleeps in a dark cage by herself.
Devours food and sips water gingerly.
Flies around in her cage occasionally.
Flapping of her wings
Sounds like the clapping of hands.
Talks in a sweet lullabye voice.

I should point out that Kurtis is a warm and empathetic writer-teacher who establishes a lot of good feelings and trust very early on, creating an atmosphere where writing about "my soul is" seems natural. He is also a student and professor of oral poetry, and someone who is comfortable with improvisation, so writing a poem in front of the class is a natural part of his teaching style. A different teacher who wanted to try this kind of poetry revision might alternatively start with, "My personality is—" or "The inside of me is—." The initial words do not need to be about deeply meaningful or personal subjects. The apprehensive teacher could also prepare the night before by writing the poem in advance and then putting the draft stages of it on the board or overhead projector.

Poet-teacher Peter Sears says of revising poetry:

See if there is any way to express the feelings even more strongly. Look for parts of the poems that could be dropped out, without really hurting the poems. As you work to trim a poem down, you will intensify its expression. Look out, though, because you can cut a poem down too much. What's too much, or not enough? That's for you to decide—and possibly a few good readers you really trust. And whatever else you do, check each word carefully. Check it for meaning and sound.[2]

_____

[2] Peter Sears, *Gonna Bake Me a Rainbow Poem: A Student Guide to Writing Poetry* (New York: Scholastic, 1990), p. 109.

Sears's point that trimming intensifies expression also applies to prose. If I'm writing a short story, between the first full draft and the final version, I typically cut away about one third of the words. I try to go through my piece (after it has sat for a while) as if I were an easily bored reader, looking for anything that doesn't make the piece more interesting. I try to pretend that someone else wrote all those words and I cut everything that doesn't seem absolutely essential.

TRY THIS: Try a Rapid Read. Go through your piece as fast as you can, looking for anything that seems remotely out of place or uninteresting. Whenever your interest as a Rapid Reader seems to flag even a little, mark the passage for possible cutting. Later, come back and read through without the marked passages. If the piece still makes sense without a marked passage, cut it.

TRY THIS: To look closely at the words, try revising by reading backwards. That is, read the last paragraph first, then read the next-to-the-last paragraph, and so on. This gives you an opportunity to get a sense of your paragraphs and sentences as individual entities. Do your sentences stand alone? They may not—after all, theoretically, everything that comes before leads up to that final sentence— but you are likely to catch repetitions or awkwardnesses that you missed in the forward flow of reading.

TRY THIS: Do a final read-through at as close to your normal reading pace as possible. Don't read at your desk, or on your computer screen, but from hard copy while sitting in your easy chair or wherever you usually read. Try not to become an editor, but stay a reader. If you can do this, anything that bothers you or stops you may well be something that would bother or stop another reader.

There is an old cartoon in which a sculptor has a visitor in his studio. The sculptor is working at a great multi-ton chunk of marble, and the visitor's question, though not stated, is obvious. "Oh," says the sculptor, "I just chip away everything that doesn't look like an elephant." I don't know how good the joke is, but the lesson here for a writer is excellent: if it isn't a part of this particular elephant—or story or poem or essay or book or line or phrase—chip it away.

But save the chips. Taking something away is not the same as destroying it, nor is it the same as saying the first version was bad or a failure. Those rejected words may have been vital to your process of working through your piece. Or, they may have been part of an idea that underlies your present idea but has been superseded. They may also be something you can use later.

Here are two little examples of the way I make cuts in my fiction. First is a short passage from a novel-in-progress (you only need to know that Susan and Dwight are married; their daughter, Fern, is a teenager; and Susan's father hasn't been answering his phone):

Earlier version

When Susan walked back into the living area, she said, "He isn't answering."

"He's in the shop fixing something," said Dwight.

Susan said, "On Sunday morning?"

"Then maybe he went to church," said Dwight.

"Oh sure," said Fern. "Grandpa's in church all right."

"You never know," said Dwight, "you never know when these old sinners are going to repent."

Trimmed-down version

When Susan walked back into the living area, she said, "He isn't answering."

"Maybe he went to church," said Dwight.

"Oh sure," said Fern. "Grandpa's in church all right."

"You never know," said Dwight, "you never know when these old sinners are going to repent."

The earlier version was not bad; in fact, it was perfectly acceptable, and perhaps even more naturalistic than the second, in the sense that people usually say more words and make more noises and gestures in real life than we conventionally transcribe in fiction. This is something to keep in mind especially when you are beginning to revise your fiction. It is even possible that in reading this tiny snippet, you prefer the longer version. However, in the context of the whole passage, of which this snippet is a part, I found that tightening the scene helped to emphasize a characteristic of Susan's—that she is depressed and laconic. So the tightening actually does two things at once: it intensifies the scene and adds information about a character. If you have any doubt about whether a sentence or dialogue exchange should be cut, ask yourself if it is doing more than one thing at once. If it isn't, it probably can be cut.

Here is another example from an unpublished novel of mine. This sample is from the novel when it was in the third person limited, before I decided to switch back to first person. I decided to cut the italicized material, an interior monologue that gives insight into the protagonist's state of mind.

> This time, the phone didn't ring, but she did stop and go back for her term paper. She thought she might as well slip it under the professor's door, since his office was in Hamilton Hall, and she was going to be there anyhow. *I shouldn't, she thought. This is just good-girl behavior, and I don't want to be a good girl when the revolution is beginning. But I don't care, it may be wrong, but I'm the kind of person who has to finish things.* She rolled the paper into a piece of cardboard, taped it shut, and tucked it into her jeans, inside her sweatshirt.

So the cut version reads like this:

> This time, the phone didn't ring, but she did stop and go back for her term paper. She thought she might as well slip it under the professor's door, since his office was in Hamilton Hall, and she was going to be there anyhow. She rolled the paper into a piece of cardboard, taped it shut, and tucked it into her jeans inside her sweatshirt.

I want to reiterate that the italicized material is not intrinsically bad. Earlier in a novel or story, for instance, you might want to convey more about the character's personality by using such material. Near end of a novel, however, the extra details slow down the action too much. In this example, I felt that the reader would simply want to know what was going to happen next.

Perhaps the single most important technique for revising is the simplest: get a distance from your writing. Separate the process from the product. Imagine the reader reading it. Imagine the toughest English teacher you ever had going over it. And if you have trouble getting distance on it, lay it aside for six months, one month, a week, a day.

TRY THIS: As an experiment, take some short passage of your writing (a page, a long paragraph) and set yourself the task of reducing the length by one-third.

TRY THIS: Try the same exercise, exchanging pieces with a friend (preferably a close one). Try to pare down the other person's piece by one third or one-half. Is it easier or harder to work on someone else's piece?

TRY THIS: Take a magazine article that has something wrong with the writing. See if you can cut it down.

TRY THIS: Especially if you are in a hurry to get out a letter or a report or some other workaday prose, hide yourself in the executive washroom or behind a tree in the park and read the whole thing aloud. This is a short cut to putting distance between you and the work, looking with a cooler eye by hearing it with your ear.

TRY THIS: Just as hearing your work by reading it aloud or tape recording it can give you the extra distance to edit better, so can the physical relationship of your eyes to the words. If you work on a computer, print out a hard copy, and revise that for a while, or if you are working on a manuscript, carry it to a higher table and work on it in a standing position for a while, so that your eyes quite literally have a different perspective, a different distance. If you are working at a computer, push your chair back so that you are farther from the screen and keyboard.

There are, of course, other considerations in polishing or closely editing your work. Are facts a problem? Are yours straight? Do you need to explain more, or have you explained too much? Fact checking is something that a knowledgeable reader can help you with and perhaps save you from embarrassment. But there is also the question of which facts are necessary and which ones might be distracting. For example:

> It was the smell of kerosene that threw her . . . farther back than she liked to remember: cold mornings somewhere—it had to be *Avenue D*—herself very small, very cold, the air at once sharp and oily.

> It was the smell of kerosene that threw her . . . farther back than she liked to remember: cold mornings somewhere—it had to be *the Lower East Side*—herself very small, very cold, the air at once sharp and oily.

Look at the change in the italicized words: this represents a distinction based on audience. *The Lower East Side* is a term many Americans might reasonably be expected to have heard of as a poor neighborhood in New York; *Avenue D*, on the other hand, is a more precise location within the Lower East Side. *Avenue D* gives some special background information to a New Yorker, but will probably mean nothing to someone in Oregon or Northumbria. Thus, the writer has to make a decision as to more or less precision for more or fewer people.

Word choice is, of course, part of the nuts and bolts of writing. In this book, I have not focused on the subject of word choice partly because everything in this book involves word choice, but also because word choice is the only thing many beginning writers think about when they think of revision. I like it best when the word choice follows naturally the other elements of deep revision, such as adding more specific information or figuring out what voice will tell your story best. There are, however, many times when looking directly at the words themselves will open up new insights for revision. Consider the following:

crazed like the rivulets under the glaze of an old piece of pottery

versus

crazed like the cracks under the glaze of old pottery.

By changing a fancy word (*rivulets*) to a simpler one (*cracks*) and cutting a few words ("an old piece of pottery" becomes "old pottery"), the writer makes the phrase shorter, easier to visualize (because it has fewer elements), and easier to read aloud— although it still does not go trippingly on the tongue. Usually I recommend greater specificity—a particular green Mexican cup, say, rather than just pottery in general—but here we are talking about elements in a simile in which too much elaboration is distracting. I wanted that pottery to be just a brief hint of a mental image. *Rivulets*—a very pretty word—calls too much attention to itself: you begin to think about water and the relative size of a creek and a brook, when what I wanted was to describe something that exists in its own right and isn't wet at all.

TRY THIS: Describe some common object as elaborately and "purpley" as you can. Then describe the object again as simply as you can, with as few words as possible. Is one style more natural to you than the other? There's no reason why you can't write both ways. In which circumstances would you write in the elaborate way? The simpler way? Is it possible to combine the two passages?

TRY THIS: If you are *not* in a terrible hurry and want to make the surface of your writing at once smoother and deeper, do some word study. As you polish, if you come across a word that is important in your writing, or has simply always intrigued you, look up its meanings and etymology. (In the course of writing this book, for example, I looked up entries on "fiction," "finish," and "malleable," all words that are important in this book, and I learned a lot.)

Another thing to look for in your word choices is stereotyping. Do you, in your nonfiction, want to include women as well as men in your grammatical forms? One approach is to think of a specific individual when you say "for example," rather than generalizing. In chapter five, I had first written:

> Some literarily sophisticated young person might slump down in his or her seat and say, "But that's what I wanted, for the reader to have some input."

I could have manipulated the words to avoid a pronoun altogether by writing:

> Some literarily sophisticated young person might say, "But that's what I wanted, for the reader to have some input."

But I kept picturing a real person as I revised this. It wasn't "he" or "she," nor was it "he or she," it was a definite student I had in mind, a young man who had been studying literary theory. I turned him into a minor character:

> Some sophisticate with a text on literary theory in the back pocket of his black jeans may say, "But that's exactly what I wanted, for the reader to make up his own mind. I want it to be the reader's decision."

One reason I often go to considerable lengths to avoid writing simply "an old lady" is because I remember that when I was fifteen, I hated to be lumped and clumped as a part of "you young people today." Therefore I give myself the task of envisioning specific individuals as much as possible in my writing examples, and by this means I limit my stereotyping.

TRY THIS: As an antidote to being too nice, try writing a stereotype or caricature. Make a brief portrait of some member of a group (rich old white Chief Executive Officers?) that is very detailed and very stereotypical. Watch out, though, for too much detail—once you start really seeing the individual, the stereotype will begin to fall apart.

Finally, if you are at the last stage of fine editing, be sure to read or show your work to a friend or a group. Other people will catch you on little details: is a flower blooming out of season? Does someone's accent sound fake? Did you repeat *limpid* three times on one page? You can get advice from other people sooner, but always be specific about what you want from them. (See chapter four for more on "Using Other People's Responses.")

TRY THIS: Ask a friend to read your piece, or read it to your class or writers' group. Then ask them the following questions:

1. Is anything confusing?
2. Do certain words seem to draw unnecessary attention to themselves?
3. Does any part go on too long?
4. Are there any facts I got wrong?
5. Do I use any clichés?
6. Do I use any stereotypes?
7. Does anything sound wrong?
8. If a stranger had written this, would you answer these questions any differently? If so, how?

TRY THIS: Do the same thing, but actually hand the friend or friends a piece of paper with the questions on it, and ask for *written* answers. (This way the friend may act more like a teacher.)

TRY THIS: Imagine the person you would like to read your poem, story, or essay actually reading it. Where is that person sitting? Is it someone in your same age group? Is the person older than you or younger? Laughing as he or she reads, or looking very serious? How would your ideal reader describe your piece to a friend? What parts does he or she like best? Write a paragraph describing the person.

TRY THIS: Try writing a review of your piece, emphasizing what's wrong with it, or a severe teacher's critique of it.

TRY THIS: Write a letter to yourself as if you were an editor considering the piece for publication. What would you say to yourself?

Dear Pamela,

Your stories are excellent mostly because of your good descriptions and how your story flows, but if I were you I would add a little bit more detail, and when you are describing a person or place give specific colors, textures, and width. The story lines and plots are very good and I would suggest you keep on writing to finish one of your pieces. My suggestion to you for finishing a piece is brainstorming about the last sentence or paragraph that you wrote. For example, in "The Girl with Clammy Hands" you left off with Jillian and the other girls going to her room on the third floor. Brainstorm on what could happen in the girls' room. Have fun writing and good luck!!!!!!!!!!!!

Sincerely,
P.B. Maxa, Editor
(Pamela James, sixth grade)

TRY THIS: Reconsider your writing by making up a dialogue in which a teacher, editor, or friend has a conversation with you about it.

JEFF: Your story is great, but there are a few details missing, like why did you look up when you went to your locker? And how did you first get to know who Chicken Fingers was?

JASON: Well, I am going to explain it in part two. When I meet him and his dog and finish them off. Also when I was by my locker the wind blew so hard that the sweat on my hands was drying up.

JEFF: Well, thank you for your comments, and I will be back for the second part.

—*Jason Hodge, sixth grade*

TRY THIS: Emily Dickinson wrote the first version of a poem (below) in 1859, and about two years later revised the second stanza. How would you change the second stanza?

Safe in their Alabaster Chambers—
Untouched by Morning
And untouched by Noon—
Sleep the meek members of the Resurrection—
Rafter of satin,
And Roof of stone.

Light laughs the breeze
In her Castle above them—
Babbles the Bee in a stolid Ear,
Pipe the Sweet Birds in ignorant cadence—
Ah, what sagacity perished here!

(version of 1859)

(For her revision, see the appendix.)

Logically speaking, polishing and editing come last, but sometimes, as you work at the surface of your writing, you will suddenly have a new sense of how it should be shaped. The trick is to be willing to follow your new impulse, even if it means making rough what you thought was finally getting smooth. And yes, if you're willing to work hard at polishing and considering the possibilities, sometimes you really can achieve a satisfactory whole, a piece that has the right word choices and makes the right decisions.

Chapter Eleven
Structuring the Longer Work

Imagine you are in the middle of revising a substantial piece of writing: a research paper, a long story, a book. You find yourself feeling stuck, lost, in a muddle. You already have a substantial pile of pages in front of you—perhaps an entire first draft—but now you are thrashing, flailing, or not moving at all. You may have an outline that tells you precisely what direction the piece will take, how it should be organized, and how it should end. You may have gone so far as to have begun polishing. But suddenly, in the middle of revision, you have to admit that more is wrong than word choice or a few paragraphs in need of recasting. The beginning is fine; you think you know how it will end; but there seems to be something wrong with the middle.

My experience, particularly with long projects, is that how well the middle works depends on the structure. Beginnings often go smoothly because of the initial inspiration and enthusiasm. Endings may exist as a goal to work toward. But the middle of a long work needs strong structural elements to support its weight. The deepest level of revision is to make or discover the structure, the central order of a work, and this often cannot be done until the work is well underway.

Problems with the middle manifest themselves in many different ways, and are often hidden at first because you believe you already have a plan. Having thought your project through carefully in advance, you may not immediately see why you are becalmed in the doldrums. You find yourself counting pages and wondering, "Do I really have as much to say as I thought I did?" or, conversely, "I've got so much stuff, it will never all come together." You lose the original impetus. You lose your enthusiasm. There is a flaccidity, a trailing off of ideas and sentences. Another symptom is that new ideas seem to exacerbate the problem because they don't fit the plan. It seems too exhausting to figure out where the new ideas go. The demands of everyday life may intervene, and you lose touch with the work, so that it seems increasingly difficult to keep struggling with revision that never seems to get anywhere. You find yourself questioning your whole project. What holds all this together, what drives it forward, and how do you get back in the driver's seat?

Sometimes you can solve the problem by doing something as mundane as reorganizing your daily life to make time for writing. It may be that as you've been away from the manuscript so long that it takes all your energy to remember what you were thinking about when you last wrote. In my novel writing classes, one of the most common complaints is that it is hard to keep going. How do you make a second draft that pushes deeper and farther when you are working nine-to-five? How do you get back to deep revision of a draft you wrote several years ago? The first step is simply to develop a routine. I know people who have developed the writing habit by writing at their offices when their colleagues are at lunch. I know a college professor who keeps her memoir-novel on a computer at her country cottage, and whenever she goes there, she revises and expands the book. Her city apartment is where she studies and reads student papers; the cottage is where she revises her book. The place itself becomes the disciplining factor.

TRY THIS: If you are having trouble with the middle of your piece, whether it is long or short, stop everything and commit yourself to a certain place and time for working on it. Regularity is essential, whether the working time is three nights a week or every morning from 6 to 7 A.M. or every Saturday afternoon or one Saturday a month. Vow to sit with the work at your chosen time whether it seems good, bad, or terrible. If you can't revise, sit and stare at the writing. The very act of being with it—the commitment to sit there and do nothing even if no ideas come—will go a long way toward regenerating your momentum.

TRY THIS: Make a written contract with yourself. Be realistic: promise yourself to revise one chapter or section every weekend, or to do a deep revision of three chapters by the end of the summer. Make part of the contract to review the contract in a certain period of time, a month or six months, and revise the contract at that time if necessary.

Another way to approach problems with the middle is to consider whether or not you really *do* have a structure that can carry the weight of your materials and ideas. When you have such a strong structure—a powerful organic shape—the middle can take on momentum and feel as inevitable as the beginning. This is true of all kinds of writing, but the longer the work, the more important this kind of structuring becomes—getting a sense of the work's own proper shape. You may therefore need to spend some time developing a general sense of the shape of what you are working on. You need a mental image of the entire work, a way of holding it in your memory. One way of doing this is to learn something about form and structure in general. Some writers find that using the form or format of a different genre helps them to structure their own work. For instance, I know a fiction writer who has published dozens of short stories and articles, but has never been able to finish a novel. Lately she has been teaching herself the longer form by co-authoring a murder mystery with a friend. This is actually a double change of pace. She says that the combination of trying to meet the requirements of the genre and of discussing it with another person are teaching her how to plot and finish her more strictly literary novel.

TRY THIS: If you are writing a story and having trouble with the climax, try learning the elements of a one-act play. You might write one, read one, or best of all, attend a few to get a sense of how the play builds, climaxes, and ends. Don't be afraid to imitate the form if it seems to fit your work. Don't worry about being derivative; your structure will probably change many times more before you are finished.

TRY THIS: If you are having trouble with finishing a long project, stop and write a short piece, perhaps a feature article for a newspaper. The experience of finishing something can help you finish your big project.

TRY THIS: Try writing in one of the genres (mystery, thriller, horror, science fiction, fantasy, romance, western), or at least reading a few and analyzing their structures.

Having a form, of course, does not necessarily mean following the pre-existing formula of some genre. Some of the best genre writing often works against its formula (e.g., the narrating detective turns out to be the murderer). Rigid adherence to a perfectly consistent pattern is not the same as having a powerful structure. Many writers, in fact, find that their structure improves when they break away from formulas or outlines, especially ones that they fixed on too early. Becoming committed to a plan too early is one of the causes of the loss of momentum in the middle. When new ideas come, there is no room for them, and the writer feels stuck or even resentful of having to stay with the plan instead of galloping free with the new ideas.

Remember that the original plan of a long work often gets supplanted during deep revision. In a lyric poem, a letter, a short story, or an essay—anything you can go through in one sitting—it is much easier to keep hold of your original sense of its shape. But in a long work—fiction, nonfiction, or long poem—you need to be ready to see a different shape underlying the work, if such an idea comes to you. The new way of looking at your work may come in one flash, or, more likely, you may need to find techniques to help you envision your work as a whole and then keep this vision in mind. The larger the project, of course, the harder it is to be able to do this, but since wholeness underlies structure, it is well worth the effort.

TRY THIS: Just for fun, close your eyes, sit back, and count back slowly from ten. When you reach zero, turn the zero into a frame or a screen, and imagine on it a creature that is your written piece. Is it a macaw? A beagle puppy? What does it look like, what does it do?

TRY THIS: Close your eyes and imagine your long project as an object. It may be only a form: a pyramid, say, or a sphere. Try to imagine its tactile qualities. Perhaps it is not a solid at all, but a fluid. Is it so large that you can swim in it? Is it contained in something else, or can you hold it? Imagine it again, but this time force yourself to envision it as something you can hold in your hand. Is it alive, hard, cold, rough, toylike, or what? Write down your images.

An orange, more like a nectarine, skin mottled, bumpy, but inside full of juice and pulp. . . .

—*Eve Blake, NYU School of Continuing Education*

*   *   *   *   *

A dull matte surface painting—lots of deep turquoise. The frame is
brass and wood and has carvings . . .

    —Koshi Bharwani, NYU School of Continuing Education

TRY THIS: Then imagine it again, this time as something
larger than you, with you inside, and explore it.

The exercises above may seem too touchy-feely or New Age to
some people, but I've found they sometimes help me and my students. Here's another one that touches the fantasy all of us have of
literary success:

TRY THIS: Imagine that your work has been published in
book form with a beautiful cover illustration. Describe that cover in
detail.

A red blotch, much like the one in Henry's stomach, with family mem-
bers looking at it, only faces.
An illness in the family.
The blotch looks like it is taking over the page.

    —Eve Blake, NYU School of Continuing Education

            *   *   *   *   *

An African-American woman in a wedding dress in the middle of the
cover with a worried, sad expression on her face. Faint images of scenes
around her. In those scenes are the men in her life.

    —Dana M. Hamilton, NYU School of Continuing Education

TRY THIS: Now imagine that your book is being published
with illustrations for each chapter. Write a description of each of the
most important illustrations. What would be emphasized in each
section of the book? Next imagine that your work has not only been
published, it has also been widely acclaimed! Write a brief version of
one glowing review, including a précis of the work that mentions at
least one small flaw.

This is a sensitive story of a young woman who finds herself. It studies questions that many today face. It is fraught with humor. Though
the book is very interesting and captivating, it could use a little more
research on the young woman's occupation as well as a more mature

plot outline. Yet all in all it was a very enjoyable and imaginative piece. Bravo Ms. Hamilton! We are looking forward to hearing more from you.

—*Dana M. Hamilton, NYU School of Continuing Education*

*　　*　　*　　*　　*

In this first novel we see the West depicted through its people rather than its stereotypes, people who laugh and love, fail and fall. Conversely, we see the characters through the eyes of circumstances, as it were. Indeed, my only objection is that the plot sometimes seems to take twists merely for the sake of character development. After generations of seeing the West depicted as stage-heroism, it is refreshing to see it populated by real people, living real lives. This realism also brings home the uniqueness of the pioneering adventure.

—*Ray Saunders, NYU School of Continuing Education*

The goal of these last two exercises is to imagine the form of your work, and thus to glimpse it as a whole, which can give you a sense of its underlying structure. Here are some other techniques that are also useful for getting a sense of the whole:

TRY THIS: Make a chronology. Especially if you are writing a feature article, or personal narrative or fiction, and even if it is something that will not be in chronological order, make a simple list of events *in* chronological order, perhaps with dates or hours. (Do this even if it is the story of one day or one hour. Do it even if you intend to ignore the usual conventions of narrative.)

TRY THIS: Try making a list of *dramatis personae,* as in the beginning of a playscript. Include the little tags stating age and one or two other salient characteristics. Then add a précis of the most important scenes.

A secondary benefit of this last exercise is that it can be a shorthand method of seeing if you might have more characters than you need, or not enough. Perhaps your three real-life brothers would work better in fiction conflated to two brothers, or even one.

TRY THIS: Try what novelist and writing teacher Suzanne McConnell has her students do: tell your novel or book in two or three minutes to a group or to a friend.

Probably the most familiar way of structuring a piece of writing is to use an outline. I particularly recommend outlining as a type of deep revision. There is no better way to get a mental image of where you have been, and ideas for where you might go. There are many methods and forms of outlining, and you can probably find one that suits you, but the most important advice I can give is this: outline *after* you have drafted. Before you do anything else, write your first page, your dramatic climax, and the lines that have been reverberating in your brain, anything that comes easily. Draft, rapidly, as much as possible. Then—when you hit the doldrums, when you begin to feel out of control with all this material—outline.

At this point, outlining is a wonderful tool. The roman numerals and sub-headings can be extremely helpful, although I am always suspicious of an outline that looks too neat. An outline is there to be scribbled on, scratched out, revised. Your drafting and revising may not follow a chart, but a chart often helps writers focus on what is really important. And—perhaps best of all—it helps you see what you have included and what you have left out.

TRY THIS: Read over what you have written so far. Write a sentence outline—a simple list of what you have, one sentence for each section or chapter. This is particularly good on a thesis-length or book-length project, but it is also good for organizing a short article or essay.

TRY THIS: Read over your drafted material and make a rough roman numeral outline of what you've written. Do not include anything that is only in your head and not on the page. Outline only what you have written. In pencil or different colored ink, put in what you hope to add in the coming weeks. That is, fill in the outline with projected writing.

TRY THIS: Try a flow chart or a cluster outline. Instead of the linear roman numeral form, use a sort of mapping of your ideas with arrows leading to other events or characters. Try to chart your ideas and where they lead. Again, look for gaps where you let something drop and consider if you want to continue it or remove it. A cluster outline is similar to a flow chart, but uses ideas grouped together in clumps, all the things that go together.

TRY THIS: Try a beat sheet. This is a term from film and television that refers to listing the events and emotional high points of each scene or section. Also from the cinema and television world is the scenario, in which instead of writing a sentence for each section or chapter, you write a brief paragraph describing the main action.

A student in my novel class invented a work-sheet outline (see figure 1). This type of format might not be for everyone, but this particular writer had been working for a long time, and had accumulated a lot of material, which he was now deeply revising. Although he had an outline sheet for each chapter, some were full of information and others had only the barest hint of what he hoped to do.

TRY THIS: Copy the worksheet form in figure 1 or make one in a form more appropriate to you. Prepare one for each chapter or section of your work. Use this new form to see where you need to fill in information.

I use various types of outlines at various times, depending on the type of project. If I have a lot of notes on a book I'm reviewing, for example, I will often sketch out only a three- or four-sentence (or phrase!) outline:

1. Describe plot
2. Why it's fun to read—a good read
3. But on the other hand—problems
4. Summary

I may never look at the outline again for such a short piece of writing (perhaps only three hundred words), because I can read the whole piece over repeatedly and get the sense of the whole that way, but as I embark on revising, the four notes give me a quick grasp of the underlying structure.

In longer projects, I use the more elaborate outlines in three ways: 1) I use them the way I do some of the exercises above—as a means of seeing my work whole; 2) I use them as a means of keeping

PART		TITLE	
		Theme/Reference	

CHAPTER		TITLE	
Time			
Setting			
Description			
of Action			
Remembrances			
Conflicts/Parallels			
Streams/Monologs			
Images/Quotations			
Research			
Notes			

Figure 1

notes on what happened in a given chapter, who appeared, etc. That is, I go back to the outline after each day's work and make changes, thus keeping a running account of the work; 3) I use the outline to make notes to myself on possible future plans for revisions.

Usually I also keep a log, separate from the outline, in which I simply note down my progress in writing and revising. I always knew, for example, that the outline for *Deep Revision* would change, and I used it to keep a record of how many pages I had so far, of potential chapter titles, and any other odds and ends that occurred to me. At the end of each writing session, I also made notes in the log: what I had accomplished that day and what I planned for the next day.

TRY THIS: For long projects, keep up a log of your work, with notes saying when you worked and more or less what you did, plus what you intend to do at your next writing session. Here are some sample entries from my log for *Deep Revision*:

July 15
I want to go over the draft of the introduction and chapter one, also go over the outtakes and either slip them in or get rid of them. Next, chapter two. This is the first day I feel like I'm really rolling.

July 16
Okay, with a lot of effort, chapter two. I'm having some doubts about organization, but I think I want to barrel on through. Pick up with chapter three.

July 17
Chapter three is cooking now. When I pick up again, backtrack a little, go over the end of chapter three. I ran out of steam at the end.

July 20
I am still working on chapter four—have an okay rough-rough. I've begun to change names of chapters. Tomorrow, finish chapter 4, be sure to erase files that have been incorporated into chapters, avoid confusion.

I think of outlining and logging as "getting-control" exercises. They are most useful, it seems to me, for keeping track of what I have written and for keeping a long work in perspective. Most often now my outlines are ever-changing, as my structure becomes clear in my mind. Here's an excerpt from my outline for this book in mid-writing. This outline does not, of course, correspond to the book as it now exists.

III. *PART THREE:* REVISING FOR FORM

Chapter Nine: Using Other Texts in Writing (Chap9)

1. Imbedded Texts
2. Literature from the Inside Out
3. Imitation (26pp)

Chapter Ten: Beginnings, Middles, and Endings (Chap10)

Beginnings as Process; Beginnings as Product
Middles; or, Structuring the Longer Work.
   a. My process in this book
     Various forms of pragmatic outlining: Backwards
     outlining, flow chart outlines; auto-contracts.
     Various exercises useful in getting a sense of a longer work such
     as a book or long paper; visualizations to precede writings; writ-
     ing blurbs; describing frontispieces and other illustrations; book
     covers; lists of illustrations; reviews and teacher's reaction; ima-
     gining your book/essay as a creature or thing; imagining your
     reader reading.
       Cutting and Polishing Is Ending
          Cutting the stone and polishing it
          Techniques for looking at your own work:
          letters from editors, etc.
          Revising the teaching of writing: some student
          opinions.

Chapter Eleven: Some completed pieces and their revisions

Note especially the difference between chapter nine, which at
that point I had completed drafting, and chapter ten, which I was
then working on. Also note that this old outline ends with the chapter that now begins the book. After one revision of the manuscript,
I took a break for a week, and then came back to it for the next draft.
As I skimmed over everything, I felt vaguely displeased with the
structure. I liked the chapter on complete pieces and how they were
revised, but something bothered me, and I wasn't sure what. I finally
realized that this chapter was really not what my book was leading
up to. Everyone has a general sense of how a piece is edited: you read
it over and say, "Oh, I like this part, how about cutting some stuff
here?" So that chapter struck me as the logical one with which to

start the book rather than to end it. This important structural decision came after I had nearly three hundred pages drafted and *partially revised*. It also came at a time when I had been away from the project. I came back, began working with my outline, and suddenly had an idea for an important restructuring.

I've described my own process of writing this book because I want to make it clear that the deepest revision is never really separate from drafting. Everything except the very first flush of inspiration (perhaps the most exciting and liberating stage) and the final editing and polishing (a kind of mature, benignly amused period for deciding to go back to "red" because "crimson" was too purple) is a process of doubling back and making changes. Revision thus happens in tandem with the drafting of new material. How can you separate the recasting of a dull paragraph from drafting new material?

This relatively well-organized approach to writing a long piece, however, is generally too neat for writing fiction, long or short. Fiction writing seems to work more under the surface: what doesn't appear at once often takes a long time to come to fruition. One of my short stories, for example, began as an outtake from a long fiction project. I found myself sidetracked one day, writing material that was tangential to the novel. I followed my instinct and wrote many pages, as if it were a part of the novel, but it seemed to have little connection to the main theme, so I made the drastic decision to cut it out of the book entirely—all fifty pages.

I finished the novel, published it, and always meant someday to get back to those fifty pages. I vaguely imagined working them up into a book, but when I sat down to try, I lost interest and put the pages back in their file. In the end, five or six years after the initial drafting of the material, I skimmed it rapidly one day and pulled out the parts I liked best. Instead of fifty pages, I suddenly had about twenty-five, and by the time I had tightened and polished, revised deeply and on the surface, I was down to about fifteen pages, a short story that satisfied me in its final distilled state.

Even so, in working on a collection of my short stories recently, I have been thinking of going over that story one more time. I'm thinking of doing a little tinkering, going just a little deeper. . . .

Appendix: Examples from Literature

**Lying in a Hammock at William Duffy's
Farm in Pine Island, Minnesota**

Over my head, I see the bronze butterfly,
Asleep on the black trunk,
Blowing like a leaf in green shadow.
Down the ravine behind the empty house,
The cowbells follow one another
Into the distances of the afternoon.
To my right,
In a field of sunlight between two pines,
The droppings of last year's horses
Blaze up into golden stones.
I lean back, as the evening darkens and comes on.
A chicken hawk floats over, looking for home.
I have wasted my life.

—*James Wright*[1]

*   *   *   *   *

**Autobiography: Or How I Grew Up
Never Vacationing at Bar Harbor in
the Summer or Palm Beach in the Winter**

Slept till noon
that first Tuesday after
high school last rites.

Mom didn't seem to mind.
Even brought me coffee
with "Heard you stirring."

By Friday, coffee was hot
and on the table. Monday,
she said, "Get you some
coffee, I'll fix breakfast."
Next, it was, "Son,

you're eighteen. Time
you found a job."

But I slept in another
week. One morning Dad
woke me up before he left
for the mill. "Get up.
Go look for work."

J & L Steel was slow then
but a small cinder block
company hired me to shovel
sand and gravel around
for wages. I came home
at four-thirty
tired and dusty
but feeling good.
I always was big
for my age, strong.

Each paycheck made life
take on brand new meaning.
For maybe two months.

That was 1950.

"Quit my job," I said
seven months later.
"Going to college."
"What for?"
"Gonna learn stuff."

Boy, what a ruckus.

"How you figure to pay?"
"Gonna enlist first.
See, they got a new war.
Korea."
"You could get killed."
"Yeah, I could."

Dad threw this in extra:
"You and hard work,
you never did get along."

And that's the story
of my whole life.

Went to war, then college.
Learned stuff.
Loved every moment.
Got married, then.
Became a teacher.
Had kids. Paid
taxes and premiums.

Kids grew up and left.
Oldest died young,
thirty. Cancer.
Other two got married.
One was arrested first.

I retired, a widower.
Two swell grandkids.
Never did win the lottery.
Finally died.

All because
one day in the rain
I'd found Robert Frost.
Him and his
two damn roads.

> —*Peter D. Zivkovic*[2]

*   *   *   *   *

216

Safe in their Alabaster Chambers—
Untouched by Morning—
And untouched by Noon—
Lie the meek members of the Resurrection—
Rafter of Satin—and Roof of Stone!

Grand go the Years—in the Crescent—above them—
Worlds scoop their Arcs—
And Firmaments—row—
Diadems—drop—and Doges—surrender—
Soundless as dots—on a Disc of Snow—

—*Emily Dickinson* (version of 1861)[3]

* * * * *

The Vulture

A vulture was hacking at my feet. It had already torn my boots and stockings to shreds, now it was hacking at the feet themselves. Again and again it struck at them, then circled several times restlessly around me, then returned to continue its work. A gentleman passed by, looked on for a while, then asked me why I suffered the vulture. "I'm helpless," I said. "When it came and began to attack me, I of course tried to drive it away, even to strangle it, but these animals are very strong, it was about to spring at my face, but I preferred to sacrifice my feet. Now they are almost torn to bits." "Fancy letting yourself be tortured like this!" said the gentleman. "One shot and that's the end of the vulture." "Really?" I said. "And would you do that?" "With pleasure," said the gentleman, "I've only got to go home and get my gun. Could you wait another half hour?" "I'm not sure about that," said I, and stood for a moment rigid with pain. Then I said, "Do try it in any case, please." "Very well," said the gentleman, "I'll be as quick as I can." During this conversation the vulture had been calmly listening, letting its eye rove between me and the gentleman. Now I realized that it had understood everything; it took wing, leaned far back to gain impetus, and then, like a javelin thrower, thrust its beak through my mouth, deep into me. Falling back, I was relieved to feel him drowning irretrievably in my blood, which was filling every depth, flooding every shore.

— *Franz Kafka*[4]

* * * * *

A Parable

Buddha told a parable in a sutra:

A man traveling across a field encountered a tiger. He fled, the tiger after him. Coming to a precipice, he caught hold of the root of a wild vine and swung himself down over the edge. The tiger sniffed at him from above. Trembling, the man looked down to where, far below, another tiger was waiting to eat him. Only the vine sustained him.

Two mice, one white and one black, little by little started to gnaw away the vine. The man saw a luscious strawberry near him. Grasping the vine with one hand, he plucked the strawberry with the other. How sweet it tasted!

Muddy Road

Tanzan and Ekido were once traveling together down a muddy road. A heavy rain was still falling.

Coming around a bend, they met a lovely girl in a silk kimono and sash, unable to cross the intersection.

"Come on, girl," said Tanzan at once. Lifting her in his arms, he carried her over the mud.

Ekido did not speak again until that night when they reached a lodging temple. Then he no longer could restrain himself. "We monks don't go near females," he told Tanzan, "especially not young and lovely ones. It is dangerous. Why did you do that?"

"I left the girl there," said Tanzan. "Are you still carrying her?"[5]

---

[1] James Wright, "Lying in a Hammock at William Duffy's Farm in Pine Island, Minnesota," *The Branch Will Not Break* (Middletown, Ct.: Wesleyan Univ. Press, 1975), p. 16.

[2] Peter D. Zivkovic, "Autobiography: Or How I Grew Up Never Vacationing at Bar Harbor in the Summer or Palm Beach in the Winter," *Dog Days,* 1992, English Department, Fairmont State College, Fairmont, WV 26554.

[3] Emily Dickinson, *The Complete Poems of Emily Dickinson,* ed. Thomas H. Johnson (Boston: Little, Brown, and Co., 1960), p. 100.

[4] Translated by Tania and James Stern in Franz Kafka, *The Complete Stories,* ed. Nahum N. Glatzer, (New York: Schocken Books, 1971), p. 442–443.

[5] These parables appear in *Zen Flesh, Zen Bones* by Paul Reps (Rutland, Vt.: Tuttle, 1957). They also appear in *The Norton Reader: An Anthology of Expository Prose,* ed. Albert Eastman (New York: Norton, 1980).

Annotated Bibliography

Atwell, Nancie. *In the Middle: Writing, Reading, and Learning with Adolescents*. Portsmouth, N.H.: Heinemann, 1987.

This popular book offers a practical method for middle school or junior high language arts classes. It is more about reading than writing, but uses writing for responding to reading in a way that helps to integrate the two.

Bernays, Anne, and Painter, Pamela. *What If?: Writing Exercises for Fiction Writers*. New York: Harper Perennial, 1990.

This book has many exercises suitable for high school and college level. These exercises are especially good for studying and revising point of view, perspective, plot, and other elements of fiction from the inside. The exercises in sections 16, 17, and 18 have a direct bearing on the revision of fiction: they help students flesh out characters that have already been drafted and sketched.

Bloom, Diane S. *Conferencing: Assessing Growth and Change in Students' Writing*. New Jersey State Department of Education, Trenton, N.J., 1986.

A nuts and bolts aid for the classroom teacher who wants to use teacher-to-student, student-to-student, and self-conferencing for revising and editing. The emphasis is on grammar and clarity. It is full of practical checklists and suggestions for classroom management. For ordering information, write to: New Jersey State Department of Education, Distribution Services, 225 West State Street, CN 500, Trenton, N.J., 08625.

Buchman, Dian Dincin and Groves, Seli. *The Writer's Digest Guide to Manuscript Formats*. Cincinnati, Ohio: Writers Digest Books, 1987.

Includes everything from t.v. scripts to illustrations and books. Handy reference work for a teacher or writer. Writer's Digest also publishes handbooks for mystery writers on subjects such as how poisons kill and law enforcement procedures, so it is worth getting on their mailing list.

Burroway, Janet. *Writing Fiction: A Guide to Narrative Craft.* 3rd ed. New York: HarperCollins, 1992.

Interesting and worthwhile for its writing suggestions, its discussion of the craft of fiction writing, and its collections of short fiction. In particular, I recommend the section called "An Example of the Revision Process," in which Burroway discusses the various drafts of a short-short story by Stephen Dunning, winner of the 1990 "World's Best Short Story Contest," on pp. 339–347.

Chatman, Seymour. *Story and Discourse: Narrative Structure in Fiction and Film.* Ithaca, N.Y.: Cornell Univ. Press, 1978.

This is an advanced discussion of the structure of narrative and how it holds steady through various media. The book gives some theoretical underpinning for my exercises in media-switching for enriching and improving writing.

Ede, Lisa. *Work in Progress: A Guide to Writing and Revising.* New York: St. Martins, 1989.

This college composition text includes a chapter on writing for an academic audience, sections on library work, and a teacher's guide. It is especially strong on interesting activities to do in groups.

Elbow, Peter. *Writing with Power.* New York: Oxford Univ. Press, 1981.

Elbow, a well-known teacher of composition, has several chapters on revision, concentrating on nonfiction. His approach is practical, excellent, and quite different from mine. I highly recommend it.

Emanuel, Lynn. "In Praise of Malice: Thoughts on Revision," *AWP Chronicle*, September 1991.

An interesting essay taking the position that poems, especially after being extensively revised, are too genteel. Emanuel makes remarks such as "In the feast of writing, revision is that dark matted lump of vegetation that leaked and wept and seemed to grow enormous on our plates at six." A good antidote for excessive rewriting.

Foxworthy, Deb J. "The Process of Revision," *Composition Chronicle*, September 1991.

An annotated bibliography of papers from various conferences.

Gensler, Kinereth, and Nyhart, Nina. *The Poetry Connection*. New York: Teachers & Writers Collaborative, 1978.

Excellent collection of contemporary poems by adults and children for use in writing workshops. Many of these poems are particularly good for imitation and for stimulating writing and discussion.

Hughes, Ingrid. "Writers' Group," *New Directions for Women*, Spring, 1979.

This fine short article describes guidelines for setting up a writers' support group. It also lists resources for women writers. Unfortunately, many of them are out of date.

Joyce, Jane Wilson. *Beyond the Blue Mountains*. Frankfort, Ky.: Gnomon Press, 1992.

A lyrical, narrative poem of great beauty that reads like a novel and is built around diary entries of women pioneers. For ordering information, write to: Gnomon Press, P.O. Box 475, Frankfort, KY 40602–0475.

Koch, Kenneth. *Rose, Where Did You Get That Red?* New York: Vintage, 1990.

The latest edition of this classic on the teaching of poetry writing. The new afterword for teachers discusses children, poetry, and revision.

Lane, Barry. *After THE END: Teaching and Learning Creative Revision*. Portsmouth, N.H.: Heinemann, 1993.

An interesting book on teaching revision in the classroom by a writer who comes out of the University of New Hampshire and the Vermont writers-in-residence program. The book focuses on establishing a vocabulary for talking about revision and on mini-lessons that lead students to revise with skill and pleasure.

Mohr, Marian M. *Revision: The Rhythm of Meaning*. Upper Montclair, N.J.: Boynton/Cook, 1984.

This book emphasizes high school and college freshman composition, and includes a somewhat dated but very full and valuable bibliography.

Murray, Donald M. *The Craft of Revision*. New York: Holt, Rinehart and Winston, 1991.

Donald Murray has been delving for many years at the grassroots of teaching writing. His specialty is demystifying and simplifying, and this small book on revision is a model of both.

Sears, Peter. *Gonna Bake Me a Rainbow Poem: A Student Guide to Writing Poetry*. New York: Scholastic, 1990.

This general guide to writing poetry is directed to students. Chapter 15 focuses on how to make poems better using various revision techniques.

Willis, Meredith Sue. *Blazing Pencils: A Guide to Writing Fiction & Essays*. New York: Teachers & Writers Collaborative, 1991.

_____. *Personal Fiction Writing: A Guide to Writing from Real Life for Teachers, Students, & Writers*. New York: Teachers & Writers Collaborative, 1984.

These are my other two books on writing, which include ideas for starting and extending both fiction and nonfiction writing. *Blazing Pencils* is aimed at middle school–lower high school kids, *Personal Fiction Writing* at older teens and adults, though many of the ideas in both books can be used at all levels.

Index of Authors

OTHER T&W PUBLICATIONS OF INTEREST

Personal Fiction Writing: A Guide for Writing from Real Life for Teachers, Students, & Writers by Meredith Sue Willis. "A terrific resource for the classroom teacher as well as the novice writer"—*Harvard Educational Review.* "Something for teachers at all levels"—NCTE editorial board.

Blazing Pencils: A Guide to Writing Fiction & Essays by Meredith Sue Willis. All you have to do is put this friendly book in the hands of junior high students or anyone looking for a wonderfully clear and practical guide to writing fiction and essays. "Can be used by students themselves or teachers . . . a fine balance between text, exercises, and examples"—*Kliatt.*

The Writing Workshop, Vols. 1 & 2 by Alan Ziegler. A perfect combination of theory, practice, and specific assignments. "Invaluable to the writing teacher"—*Contemporary Education.* "Indispensable"—Herbert R. Kohl.

Like It Was: A Complete Guide to Writing Oral History by Cynthia Stokes Brown. This how-to guide was written by a teacher who won the American Book Award for her work in oral history. For students 12 and up and for English, social studies, and history teachers. "A solid, well-organized introduction, covering everything"—*Booklist.*

The Teachers & Writers Handbook of Poetic Forms, edited by Ron Padgett. A clear, concise guide to 74 different poetic forms, their histories, examples, and how to use them. "A treasure"—*Kliatt.*

The Whole Word Catalogue, Vols. 1 & 2. T&W's best-selling guides to teaching imaginative writing. "*WWC 1* is probably the best practical guide for teachers who really want to stimulate their students to write"—*Learning.* "*WWC 2* is excellent . . . Makes available approaches to the teaching of writing not found in other programs"—*Language Arts.*

◆

For a complete catalogue of T&W books, magazines, audiotapes, videotapes, and computer writing games, contact:
Teachers & Writers Collaborative
5 Union Square West
New York, NY 10003–3306
(212) 691-6590